Lyrisa Blooms

THE SEASONAL FLOWER REVOLUTION

Lyrisa Blooms

Every garden has a story to tell, a tale of beauty, growth, and the wonders of nature. As you embark on this journey, may your hands be guided by the whispers of the plants, and may your heart be filled with the joy of creating a blooming haven that enchants both the eye and the soul

- Lyrisa Blooms-

CONTENTS

Introduction 9

CHAPTER 1: Extending the Flowering Season 11

The Foundation of Successful year round blooming 14

CHAPTER 2: Soil Preparation and Fertilization Techniques 39

Fertilization techniques 47

CHAPTER 3: Innovative Cultivation Methods 50

Successional Planting..50

Benefits of Successional Planting...............................51

Cold Frames 53

Benefits of Cold Frames 53

Indoor Gardening..55

CHAPTER 4: Extending the Flowering Period Through
Microclimate 60

Power of Greenhouse 65

CHAPTER 5: Unveiling Unique Flower Varieties 68

Incorporating Wild and Native Flowers into The Garden...73

Exotic Species for Year-Round Blooming.........................78

CHAPTER: 6: Designing For Continuous Blooms.................83

Designing for Year-Round Blooms. 84

How to Design Flower Beds and Borders 90

How to Incorporate Perennials and Annuals into Your Garden? 94

CHAPTER 7 How to Nurture and Care for Your Year-Round Blooming Garden 98

Essential Watering Techniques and Irrigation System 99

Watering techniques 99

CHAPTER 8: Pruning Strategies For Extended Flowering .. 108

Benefits of Pruning for Year-Round Blooming 113

Pruning Techniques for Different Flower Varieties 119

Step-by-Step Instructions for Pruning Flower Varieties: ... 121

Timing and Frequency of Pruning 122

Spring-Flowering Plants: 123

Summer-Flowering Plants: 123

Fruit Trees: 123

Hedges and Topiaries: 123

Pruning Dos and Don'ts: 125

Dos: 125

Don'ts: 126

Maintaining Balance: 127

CHAPTER 9: How to Protect Your Garden from Pest & Diseases? 129

How to Maintain Healthy Soil and Nutrient Balance 135

Protect the Soil with Organic Mulching 138

CHAPTER 10: Step-by-step Guide and Inspirations 143

Step-by-step Guide to Year-round Success 143

CHAPTER 11: Creating Your Personalized Year-Round Blooming Haven 155

How to Overcome Challenges and Celebrate Your Success 158

Creating Captivating Color Combinations......................... 167

Seasonal floral arrangements that showcase the potential for year-round blooming 172

Step-by-step tutorials for creating stunning bouquets, centerpieces, and other floral designs specific to each season. 178

Spring Bouquet:.. 178

Summer Centerpiece: 179

Autumn Wreath: 180

Winter Table Arrangement:.. 181

Tips for Choosing Flowers, Arranging Techniques, and Creative Ideas for Seasonal Floral Designs 183

Selecting the Perfect Flowers:... 183

Arranging Techniques: 184

Creative Ideas for Seasonal Elements: 185

Conclusion.. 187

REFERENCES 189

INTRODUCTION

Our daily lives depend heavily on floral harvests, used for everything from food and medicine to aesthetic purposes. Due to the widespread usage of flowers and flower-related items for special occasions and everyday needs, the floriculture sector has a considerable economic impact on the world. As a result, a significant percentage of the scientific community is working to develop new floriculture crops to suit the constantly expanding need for flowers in many spheres of life.

Seasonal blooming occurs at a certain time of year every year and is the set pattern by floriculture crops. As a result, some of the most stunning blooms are only visible for a brief period of time. The most sought-after flowers in the world, orchids, are notable because they often blossom after a lengthy period of time (generally two to three years). Crops that have the potential to bloom constantly throughout the year are preferred in the floriculture sector and have greater market success.

The finest program for revolutionizing the ongoing availability of the most valuable floriculture crops may be found in studies on the genetic foundation of continuous blooming patterns and its implementation in seasonal flowering crops. Research on the molecular control of continuous blooming in essential floriculture crops like roses and orchids has only recently started. In addition to providing a forum for the scientists studying floriculture to gather knowledge and apply it efficiently as they develop plans for the coming revolution of continuous blooming, this collection intends to showcase the latest research and advancements.

The application of this information to the seasonal blossoming of floricultural crops is encouraged in studies focused on the regulatory mechanisms of continuous flowering in floricultural crops. With flourishing botanical projects, the Slow Flower movement is gradually spreading to southern Europe from the field to the vase. It's a fantastic treat for floral designers seeking genuine blossoms with personality, flaws, and aroma.

CHAPTER 1: EXTENDING THE FLOWERING SEASON

We go back to the movement's beginnings and explore the energy that is bringing together designers and growers with the help of American author Debra Prinzing, one of the pioneers of the Slow Flower movement in the US, Erin Benzakein, the brains behind the American flower farm Floret, and Terry & Katie from the London-based floral studio Worm. Everything seems to have begun in 2007 with the release of "Flower Confidential: The

Good, the Bad, and the Beautiful" by American author Amy Stewart. The author investigated the globalized floral business from Holland to California and Ecuador, exposing the despicability of a society based on low-cost flowers, pollution, and unjust working conditions. By establishing connections between farmers, florists, retailers, and consumers, the initiative —which she refers to as an "inclusive community"—aims to encourage a short floral supply chain.

The Slow Flower movement, a true bottom-up movement, owes a lot to the increase in social media use, which greatly aided its quick and spontaneous development. It spread to Australia and the UK after starting in the US. Instagram has developed as the preferred platform for the movement and has significantly contributed to its development. It is rich in seed-to-field-to-vase photographs from amateur farmers to professional floral designers, such as the Edinburgh-based botanical firm PYRUS. Perhaps, as flower grower Erin Benzakein explains, this is because "seasonal flowers have a story," a tale about getting back in touch with nature that resonates with many.

People are curious about the origins of their flowers. People appreciate it when we can describe a flower's history, whether cultivated on a farm in Cornwall or has been drying in our studio since September. This enhances its uniqueness. One way Terry and Katie have discovered to get through the winter is to save energy by drying plants since the cold weather makes it a little less inspiring flower-wise unless you are buying from abroad. For instance, most of our Christmas decorations include dried flowers from warmer months mixed with local pines, according to them.

The two Irish-born artists say they are drawn to "the simplicity in how something as important as a blossom branch can be appreciated as a floral design" and do their best to exclusively utilize locally-grown botanicals. They explore seasonality and ephemerality in their arrangements by combining bundles of poppy pods with honesty flowers. Their creations often contain sculptural forms of colored palm fronds and fluffy natural grasses. They are shown in various delicate pastels, from powder pink to light green. Looking at the labor and dedication of all these practitioners, from growers to designers, we see the start (or evolution?) of a seasonal flower revolution. This huge shift influences how we see consumerism and attractiveness and is driven mostly by women. If you have a year-round garden, your house will be surrounded by color and intrigue throughout the year. No matter where you live, it is possible to have a beautiful garden even in the winter.

The Foundation of Successful year round blooming

Flowers make any landscape more beautiful. But there are a few things to know about designing a flowerbed for maximum impact. Considering these concepts, even beginners can create a bloom-filled yard that looks pro-level. One of the most enjoyable things you can do is to start a garden. Everyone can benefit from getting their hands a bit muddy by planting flower bouquets with a delightful scent or by beginning a food garden (or both!). But it might be challenging to know where to begin if you're new to gardening. However, it doesn't have to be difficult; if you divide your task into doable pieces, you can get into gardening at your own pace. Your hard work will soon be rewarded with stunning vistas, mouthwatering flavors, and vibrant blossoms. Every garden tells a tale through its flowers and layout, expressing the owner's personality and sense of style while appealing to our emotions and desires. They convey the narrative of inventiveness, discovery, aspiration, and the development of values. It's a chance to surround oneself with special memories and discoveries in addition to your favorite plants. There are many ways to make your garden look its best and reach its full potential this summer.

The instructions listed below will assist you in knowing your garden's potential and getting started from scratch, but if you have a specific idea in mind, a garden plan may also serve as a design blueprint.

- Consider What to Plant

Do you aim to grow a garden of herbs, vegetables, or a floral lawn? Plant herbs and vegetables that your family will eat or be open to trying if you want them to contribute to your supper menu. Choose between annuals, which bloom most of the summer but need replanting every spring, and perennials, which bloom for a shorter period but come back year after year, if you prefer flowers for their color, flair, and scent. Each one, or perhaps a mix, creates a beautiful landscape but will demand a different level of care. Begin simply until you understand what you're getting into.

- Select the Best Garden Location

  Most blooming plants and almost all vegetables need 6 to 8 hours a day of full light. You must watch it throughout the day to determine whether areas of your yard get full sun vs. partial or complete shadow. Most of your yard may be shaded, but don't panic; although outdoor ferns and hostas can't thrive in shadow, many other plants can. To determine how much light a plant needs, see the plant tags or speak with your neighborhood garden shop staff. If feasible, choose a generally level area for your garden since managing a sloping garden is more difficult, time-consuming, and sometimes costly. A water supply should be accessible to your new garden as well.

- Prepare the Ground

  In the area where you want to plant, get rid of sod and weeds. Cut it out if you want results immediately, as if it's already spring and you want beautiful flowers this summer. Use a spade to cut through the sod. To make it simpler to remove, cut the sod into chunks.

The lasagna gardening technique is simpler for a longer-term project: Five newspaper sheets should cover your future garden; if your lawn has Bermuda or St. Augustine grass, double that amount. On the newspaper, apply a 3-inch layer of compost (or a mix of potting soil and dirt). After watering everything, wait. The paper and compost will disintegrate in approximately four months. But if you start in the autumn, you'll have a planting area ready by spring with lots of rich soil and no grass or weeds.

• Examine and enhance your soil

Have your local cooperative extension office perform a soil test to learn more about the soil. They will guide you through the procedure: how much dirt to collect from which areas of the garden and when to take your samples are essential considerations. The results should take two weeks to reveal what your soil needs and how to improve it. You may also use a DIY kit, which might not be as comprehensive but will give you a general understanding of the nutrient levels in your soil.

Almost always, residential soil needs improvement, particularly in new buildings where the topsoil may have been removed. In addition to lacking vital plant nutrients, the soil may be compacted or have poor drainage. Usually, the solution is simple: use plenty of organic materials. Add two to three inches of compost to the soil as you dig or till a new bed. If you choose not to dig or work with an existing bed, leave the organic materials on the surface; they will eventually decompose into humus. Earthworms will do most of the work of incorporating humus into the subsoil.

- Set out your flower beds

Before planting or sowing in new beds, loosen the soil to make it easier for roots to develop and reach the nutrients and water they need. There are two techniques: manual digging or mechanical tilling with a rototiller or another tool. When you need to mix in a lot of amendments, the first one is a suitable technique.

However, going overboard is simple, which may harm the soil's structure. Smaller beds are easier to organize by digging.

In any case, work the soil when it is damp enough to form a loose ball in hand and dry enough to crush when dropped. Digging in too wet or too dry soil is harder and might damage the earth's structure. Gradually move the upper 6 to 8 inches of soil with a spading fork or spade while simultaneously incorporating the organic material from Step 4. Since walking on the organized beds compacts the soil, temporarily putting down plywood planks might help distribute the weight evenly.

• Choose Your Plants

Some spend months poring through catalogs, while others visit the garden store and purchase what impresses them. Both methods are effective if you choose plants suitable for your soil, climate, and sunshine. Even searching for plants to buy online is possible. Here are some beginner-friendly plants: Cosmos, Calendula, geraniums, marigolds, impatiens, and zinnias are examples of annuals. Black-eyed Susans, lamb's ears, daylilies, pansies, purple coneflowers, phlox, and Russian sage are some examples of perennials.

• Commence planting

You can plant certain plants in the fall or late winter since they can withstand cold temperatures, including pansies and kale. Conversely, tomatoes and most annual flowers enjoy warm weather, so wait to plant them until the risk of frost has passed in your region. Planting perennials is best done in the middle of spring and the middle of fall. The seeds of many annuals may be planted directly in the garden and are simple to cultivate. If you're a risk-taking beginner, start the growing season early by planting seeds inside a few weeks before the final day of frost. Garden stores provide flats or pots made specifically for seedlings as well as soil mixtures for them. If you don't have window space, put the pots under grow lights or on a sunny ledge according to the directions on the seed packaging. The seeds and seedlings must be kept damp but not wet to prevent rot.

- The Right Time for Water

Never let seedlings dry up; water them often. As the plants get bigger, they ebb and flow. Until their roots take hold, transplants also need regular watering (every other day or so). Following that, the watering frequency depends on humidity, soil, and rainfall; however, once per week is a decent starting point. You won't need to water your garden as often since clay soil dries up more slowly than sandy soil. Soil dries up quicker in windy, sunny circumstances than in cool, gloomy ones. Still uncertain? 3-4 inches below the surface, feel the earth. Water is needed if the soil seems dry. Water is applied slowly and thoroughly so that it soaks in rather than evaporates. Water in the morning to reduce evaporation.

- Use Mulch to Protect Your Garden

Mulch the soil with a few inches of mulch to help keep the pests out and moisture in. You will not need to water as often, and by protecting the soil from sunlight, you'll prevent the germination of weed seeds. Make sure not to cover any seeds you want to sow with mulch, or they may not even sprout. Choose from a broad range of mulches, each with advantages, such as straw, river stones, and chopped-up bark. The soil will be nurtured when the organic protection decays, such as compost, bark, or cocoa bean shells (they also smell wonderful). Choose a mulch that breaks down in a few months for a vegetable garden or a bed of annual plants. For perennial plants, use a covering that will stay longer, like bark chips.

- Regularly maintain the garden

Keep your attention on the garden tasks as your garden starts to expand to ensure that it reaches its full potential. Don't let the plants dry up; water them. Remove weeds before they bloom.

Discard any sick, infected, or dead plants. Pick them off the plant and put them into a pail of sudsy water, hose them off, or spray on an insecticidal detergent you can buy at a garden shop to get rid of damaging insects (like tomato hornworms). Use a trellis, a stake, or a tepee to support tall plants (like tomatoes). Vegetables should also be harvested as soon as they are ripe. Also, don't forget to pause and take a whiff of whatever it is you're cultivating. No matter how large your outside area is, a short clean-up will make it seem bigger. By cutting back any hedges, shrubs, or beds that may have gotten a bit out of hand during the winter, you may give the appearance of having a spacious and elegant garden. Existing plants have the greatest chance of flowering again in the summer if pruned in the spring.

How to Create a Year-Round Blooming Plan?

Are you trying to create a garden that flowers season after season with ease? Regardless of your hardiness zone, there are a few things you can do to ensure your garden produces an abundance of flowers. Never-ending blooming gardens with year-round appeal are not created by chance. A well-planned garden requires forethought and patience. It takes time to develop.

In many cases, it doesn't happen within a single season. The key to creating a garden that is continuously in bloom is to start with a plan. It's crucial to have a variety of different blooming plant species. Depending on your goals and planting schedule, you may choose either annual flowers or perennial flowers. We have compiled a list of my best suggestions to maintain vibrant, lovely blooms in your yard all season long. Choose a few plants based on their blossoms, then consider the other plants and make your selections based on the tags attached to them. Additionally, certain plants that you might buy from nurseries will bloom at the wrong time. They may have had a head start on the season by being cultivated in a greenhouse. If the plant is perennial, it will bloom the following season at the right time for your zone. While establishing a garden is not very strenuous, creating a four-season garden requires more effort. Your house will be surrounded by color and intrigue throughout the year if you plan for year-round gardening.

Create an annual garden planner before starting your garden to list the plants that will bloom each season. In addition to keeping track of what you have planted, you can also include images, comments on your garden, and other ideas in the planner.

Selecting the right plants for your location is necessary to design year-round gardens. For these all-season flower gardens, you can use any combination of perennials, annuals, and container plants, depending on your location. Although it is somewhat easier for Southern gardeners to achieve a diversity of color throughout the season, northern gardeners can still create interest and color throughout the year by using plants with intriguing leaves or other attributes. Knowing which plants thrive in your area and when they display their best can help you create a year-round garden that is both beautiful and productive. The ideal strategy for achieving harmony in a four-season garden is to choose at least two plant varieties that will bloom simultaneously during each season.

You might develop four-season container gardens in addition to year-round flower gardens. For individuals who reside in milder areas, they are a fantastic choice. Additionally, containers are a great option to bring color to your landscape year-round. Using annuals in containers offers a versatile approach, and appealing perennial or evergreen plants may also thrive in containers. In a mixed container display, spring-blooming bulbs may be combined with fall and summer-blooming plants to bring color far into the chilly season. Four-season container gardens also allow you to switch up your plants as the seasons change.

The choices of seasonal plants will give you a sense of what a four-season garden may look like, even though your choice of plants will vary based on your area and how much sunshine your garden gets. When possible, it is always preferable to use native species. If you need assistance choosing which plants to use, you can get advice from the nearest Cooperative Extension Office.

For a splash of color after a long winter, put flowering bulbs and other spring-blooming plants in your garden's spring area. These may include Tulip, Crocus, Snowdrop, Daffodil, Peony, Pansy, Forsythia, and other spring-flowering shrubs that provide color to larger landscaping areas in the spring.

Summer flowering flowers have a broad range and outstanding blooming power. While hardy camellias and other winter-loving plants are available to southern gardeners, northern gardens benefit from evergreen hollies, chokeberry shrubs, and firethorn that provide beautiful berry displays all winter. Snowdrops and hellebores, two very early bloomers, can withstand a little frost and snow and are often observed emerging on a snowy day at the end of winter.

Listed below are some important points for you to consider before planning a year-round blooming garden.

- Make springtime plans in the fall.

The finest spring gardens are sown in the autumn. We'll buy and sow spring bulbs in the autumn. Bulbs planted in the autumn produce some of the perennials that bloom the earliest. Snowdrops, Crocus, and hyacinths are a few of the often-used options. Put them in the ground in the autumn for blooming in the early spring.

- Dividing the seasons

The normal four seasons are spring, summer, autumn, and winter. But when it comes to perennial flowers, you can divide the summer and spring seasons. Your fall-planted bulbs begin to emerge and blossom in the early spring. Consider introducing hepatica and helleborcs to your garden as winter-early spring blooms. Two bushes that bloom early are forsythia and cherry blossoms. The garden is at its best in late spring. The large garden perennials are in flower at this time. This includes peonies, oriental poppies, and iris. When the explosion occurs, you typically don't have to worry too much about acquiring blooms at this time. Your spring garden changes into a summer garden in the early summer. Because the next group of flowers is often in great abundance in gardens, this transition normally occurs rather smoothly. This includes hydrangea, lavender, Shasta daisy, and delphinium.

After all the summer flowers have faded, late summer occurs. Some preparation is necessary at this time of year. There are many possibilities for the end of summer; just remember to incorporate them into the garden. Joe Pye weed, bugbane, and coneflowers are some of my favorite late-summer flowering plants that are also rather powerful.

- Avoid Ignoring Fall Blooms

Don't overlook autumn now that summer and spring have been discussed. Fall doesn't signal the end of gardens. Be certain to be interested in the autumn. You may also utilize plants with colorful leaves that change with the seasons. The monarchs of autumnal foliage are maples. But keep in mind that certain perennials, like Virginia Creeper, can lose their color in a flash.

- Put in Long-Blooming Perennials

There are several gorgeous perennials that have a somewhat limited lifespan, like the peony. Perennials, on the other hand, appear to live forever. The structure and fascination endure even after the early bloom is gone. Daylily, 'Stella D'oro,' is a fantastic, long-lasting perennial. Once it begins to bloom, it will do so throughout the summer for several weeks. The color of lavender will remain blue-purple all summer long. Coneflowers will persist throughout the autumn from late July. The robust blooms will bloom and last for months in a lovely state. The blooming shrub 'Annabelle' hydrangea is excellent. The enormous white balls of blooms will remain beautiful for months. Both globe thistle and sea holly may be left in a garden for months. After their first bloom, the spiky, highly structured blooms remain vibrant and undamaged for weeks.

- Plant many types of the same perennials.

This works with certain perennial plant varieties. Peonies are the ones that first spring to mind. They are among the garden's most beautiful and fleeting blossoms. The blooming period of a peony may be prolonged, to some extent. Different varieties have different blooming times. One of the first peonies to bloom is the fern-leaf variety. They become active and blossom in early spring. Utilizing different perennials makes this feasible. Similar to asters, irises, delphiniums, and daylilies. To make it seem as if your flowers are blooming for a longer duration, do some research to determine whether the types are early, mid, or late, and then stagger the various sorts.

- Fill your beds up

This is a personal opinion, but I like a full flower bed. But it makes sense to fill the beds if you want anything to blossom constantly. To have purple lollipops of allium bloom when the hostas are barely budding, you can plant allium bulbs in the hosta beds in the autumn. Make sure to have plants that will swath the already-blooming tulips in foliage. Using columbine or lady's mantle as perennials is preferable to fill in the gaps left by spring bulbs that wither away by summer. Planting plants that will vanish by summer is best done in a river or wave instead of a block. As a result, you won't have a large bald space in your garden, and other plants will be able to blossom and fill in the nature around them. You can plant a blue river snake through your garden using grape hyacinths. Then it disappears and is replaced by other plants.

- Pick Plants That Die Beautiful

Plants that can withstand the winter and continue to look interesting, if not gorgeous, are attractive. Therefore, choose plants whose skeletons won't decompose. Beautiful perennials include peonies, hostas, and delphiniums. However, when the cold strikes after flowers have finished blossoming, they turn to mush. For the sake of the beauty during their season, you must be prepared to accept a few dead, mushy plants in your garden. But make sure to have some perennials, and you should keep them up throughout winter to contribute to the winter landscape. The real bones of a garden are undoubtedly trees and shrubs, but some excellent perennial alternatives look gorgeous long after blooming. Silver Russian sage has lavender-purple, almost shimmering blossoms. It appears beautiful when it blooms in the summer, but throughout the autumn and winter, it simply seems to freeze in place.

Don't overlook seasonal flowers.

Utilizing annuals in the garden can help it remain perpetually in bloom.

You may incorporate annual flowers into the landscape in a variety of ways. Your flowers will last longer into the autumn since many annual flowers have extended bloom periods. A wonderful approach to smoothly incorporate flowers into your yard is to plant containers full of annuals. You may choose the color combination you prefer and experiment with creating a focal point this way, adding vibrant accent colors to your landscape.

Another choice is border annuals. This entails lining the front of a garden bed with annual plants. This creates a lovely, clean border of flowers and works well with wax begonias, pansies, impatiens, or alyssum.

Another approach is to scatter annuals among your beds. This works well to fill in gaps in your garden or to make room for large, striking blooms. Larger flowering annuals like tuberous begonias and geraniums work well for this purpose, making the blooms visible from a distance.

- Observe and Record

Gardening is a test of patience. It's not a project that you can finish quickly. Take note of any inconsistencies you observe in your garden. Note any times when the flowers aren't in bloom. You can enhance your garden for the next year by keeping a small notepad nearby where you can make notes and evaluate them.

Look through your notes before visiting a garden or nursery store to choose plants that will fill any gaps in your bloom cycle. Take a stroll while taking pictures or making notes.

- Plants in Groups

You can plant perennials in groupings of three, five, or seven. Odd numbers have more aesthetic appeal. Group planting will enhance the effect. If only one of each flowering item is present, I believe gardens will seem crowded and busy. It's bolder to add groupings of plants. Try planting 3–5 clusters of the same plant across a garden border for an even greater effect. As a result, your landscape will be covered in a wave of consistent color.

- Flowering Trees and Shrubs

To enhance the appeal of blooms, don't forget about flowering plants and trees. It's always wonderful to add flowering plants and fruit trees. They bear fruit in the autumn and bloom in thespring. Look for cultivars that don't produce large fruits or berries if you don't like picking fruit or dealing with the mess. Rhododendrons and lilacs are just two examples of the many choices available for blooming trees and shrubs that don't provide fruit. They are the shining lights of the garden when in bloom. Consider other appealing qualities besides tree and shrub blossoms, such as lovely berries or vivid autumn foliage.

- Layer with Roses

Roses that are in good health and well-maintained will bloom year-round. To encourage blooming, be sure to deadhead and fertilize them. Maintaining the bloom of your garden is simple with roses. Pruning is not that difficult once you get the hang of it. There are rose varieties available for all zones, so all gardeners can enjoy roses.

- Utilize Multiple Levels

Utilize all levels in a beautiful landscape. Incorporate low-lying ground covers, shorter perennials, taller perennials and shrubs, and finally, trees and vines in the suggested order. Utilizing all of these levels will increase the chances of flowering. Additionally, it provides depth, enhancing the charm and intrigue of your landscape. You may enjoy having many things flowering simultaneously at various stages. For instance, while larger lilac trees are in bloom, creeping thyme creates a purple carpet of blossoms. The garden's mid-range may not be in bloom at that time, but that's okay.

How to Select the Right Flower Varieties for the Garden?

Knowing which plants thrive in your area and when their displays are at their finest can help you create a year-round garden that is both beautiful and productive. The ideal strategy for achieving harmony in the four-season garden is to choose at least two plant varieties that will bloom concurrently during each season.

Your house will be surrounded by color and intrigue throughout the year if you have a year-round garden. No matter where you live, it is possible to have a beautiful garden even in the winter. Planning and preparation are needed when creating a four-season garden, even if planting the garden is not the most difficult component. Tour nurseries and gardens all year round.

You should investigate before preparing a garden bed or buying a plant. Picking acceptable plants for your area is a simple approach to start your investigation. Native plants, in particular, are advantageous since they have evolved to live in your region. Combining annuals, perennials, and container plantings for year-round color is possible when you are aware of the hardiness range of the plants in your area.

To get a feel for flowering cycles, leaf color, and which specific plants you are interested in appearing all year round, visit garden centers and gardens at various seasons.

- Examine your Garden

The fact that a plant may grow in your area does not guarantee it will flourish in your garden. For your garden to be successful, you must know which way it faces, how dry or moist the soil is, how much light it receives throughout the year, and whether or not pests or animals will be a problem. After you have the answers to these questions, you can choose the right plants for your yard.

- Remember the Foliage

Flowers are great, but they need a good environment. This is crucial for gardeners who live in regions with harsher winters. However, you do not need to use evergreens when choosing plants for background texture and winter hardiness. Many plants that shed their leaves have colorful branches and early spring blooms; some even have distorted stems or peeling bark that looks lovely in winter landscapes.

The many leaf hues available throughout the year give your landscape a ton of variety and intrigue. Using foliage in purple, green, and chartreuse colors in the garden is just as effective as using flowers.

- Purchase perennials

Annuals cost less; perennials cost more. Although they come back year after year with correct care, they will pay off in the long run. The foundation of your garden should be made of perennial plants. Filling in with annuals will increase the amount of color and intrigue. Many perennials, including coneflowers, salvias, black-eyed Susans, and daylilies, produce many blooms or a long bloom season. Plant a wide range of plants that will bloom at various periods. This will guarantee that you have a variety of gorgeous blooms scattered throughout your vibrant leaves for most of the year.

- Continue Maintenance

Your garden will benefit greatly from gardening techniques, including weeding, mulching, watering, and fertilizing. The most crucial element of a healthy landscape is mulch because it nourishes plants as it decomposes, maintains moisture at the roots, kills weeds, warms in the winter, and cools in the summer.

Don't be afraid to leave some dried flowers alone, either. Using "spent flowers" is a fantastic way to add interest and vibrancy to a winter garden. Spent flowers and grasses also provide food and shelter for birds and other overwintering pollinators.

- Monitor your garden.

Learn about the growing conditions in your garden, beginning with your hardiness zone, before making any purchases. Observe more to comprehend its brightness. Where is the midday shade? Where does the scorching sun beam all day? Do you have any areas that get little to no direct sunshine? Additionally, remember that the sun's angle varies throughout the year, along with the growth and decay of deciduous trees' leaves.

- Blend it up

You'll need to choose a variety of flora from several plant groups to cover all seasons. Shrubs, trees, and bulbs provide some of the greatest blooms during late winter and early spring. Flowers thrive among perennials and annuals throughout the spring, summer, and autumn. Although widespread in warm areas, winter flowers are unusual for northern gardeners. Fruits and vegetation with vibrant colors may fill the emptiness.

- Beyond flowers

Beyond flowers, gardens are attractive. Other intriguing features provided by plants are the color and texture of the leaves, the variety of sizes and shapes, the unique branch structure, motion in the wind, the draw of animals, and the aromas of the flowers and foliage. Remember these and other appealing components as you create your year-round landscaping.

- Get motivated

Visit parks, public gardens, and garden supply stores to get ideas. Take a picture and bring any unusual plants you come across to your neighborhood garden center for assistance with identification. Make sure your pictures are sharp and include details like the size and form of the whole plant, close-ups of the flowers or leaves, etc. They may be able to order it for you if they don't already have it in stock.

CHAPTER 2: SOIL PREPARATION AND FERTILIZATION TECHNIQUES

Soil may be taken for granted quite easily. Many of us choose a flower we wish to plant, create a hole in the ground, drop the flower in, and wait for it to sprout. This may be effective if you have exceptional soil, but for the majority of us, changing our soil is necessary to achieve the best possible growing conditions. How do you improve soil, then? To determine exactly what your soil needs and doesn't need, the first and most crucial step is to do a soil test. Learn all there is to know about soil, that dark, earthy substance. You'll discover how to get a soil test as well as what to do with the findings. This section will provide advice on how to modify the nutrients and pH of your soil to make it as fruitful as possible, regardless of whether the soil is nutrient-poor sand, heavy clay, or anything in between. The first step to a great garden is having good soil. However, the loose, black soil that makes up the beautiful gardens you see in magazines or on television is seldom an accident. Gardeners who improve their natural soils produce it.

There are many different varieties of soil, ranging from perennially dry, nutrient-poor sand to soil that is 90% rocks and 10% dirt held together to rich, heavy clay (which, when wet, creates a slippery, sticky, shoe-grabbing mass before drying to brick hardness). Fortunately, the majority of soil conditions lie in between these two extremes. However, only a few homeowners discover they have the appropriate "rich garden loam" to work with. Sand may be added to soil to make it looser and drier, while clay can make it moister and harder. To enhance texture and structure, they may be fed copious amounts of organic material, such as decayed leaves, ground-up twigs, rotting cattle manure, and old grass clippings. Any soil is nourished by organic matter, which promotes greater plant development. By getting your soil tested, you can determine the conditions of your garden in the first stage..

- Find out if you have light, sandy, productive, moderate, or heavy clay soil by testing your soil or conducting your tests. Test the soil before you begin fertilizing and amending the soil in your garden. This is in accordance with the proverb, "If it isn't broken, don't fix it." Unnecessary changes to soil acidity or nutrients may do more harm than good. A plant-based equivalent of the nutritional tables on packaged goods, soil testing reveals the quantities of nutrients in your soil. They also include organic content and P (phosphorus), two elements crucial for good overall performance from the start. Call your local Cooperative Extension Service, often listed under state or county government in the phone book, to get your soil tested. Ask them where you can get a soil-testing kit with a bag for collecting dirt and instructions. For accurate results, strictly adhere to the instructions.

The findings could appear as a chart with a lot of data, which might initially seem daunting. However, if you pay close attention to the following, you might start to analyze these figures:

- The garden requires more compost if the level of organic matter is less than 5%.

- The different nutrients will be stated, potentially in parts per million. They may also have medium, high, or low degrees of availability. You should apply fertilizer to the soil to compensate for any low-concentration elements. The pH of the soil measures how acidic the soil is. Acidic soils have ratings lower than 7. The most fertile pH range is between 6 and 7, which is somewhat acidic. Above pH 7, the soil is alkaline or basic, which might be problematic. Soils that are either acidic or very alkaline can be treated to make them more balanced and fruitful.

- Before starting a new garden, till or shovel a thick layer of compost into gently damp (never wet) soil to reactivate it. Breaking the dirt with a shovel is vital if you begin with hard, compacted soil. As you go around, dig out weed roots and other unpleasant plants. Use a rototiller to go over the soil, and after the first pass, go over it crosswise to break the dirt into manageable bits.

- Your well-tilled soil may initially seem fantastic, much like screened topsoil, but clay or silt soils are likely to become stiff, crusty, and hard after a few significant downpours. The best technique to maintain loose, light soil is to include organic materials.

- Compost should be added to the soil in a 4- to 6-inch layer and worked down to a depth of 10 to 12 inches (more if the soil is extremely poor). Before your eyes, the earth will transform remarkably, becoming darker, wet, and bouncy. The soil is likely to be loose if organic matter is present. To maintain the appropriate texture, add organic matter such as compost, mulch, or chopped leaves, as it gradually decomposes.

- Sandy soils will crumble, and they might feel rough. Apply and mix a layer of compost up to several inches thick and even a thin coating of clay before trying again to improve the sandy soil. The ball will stick together better after the soil has been treated.

- Clay soils will compact into a tight ball that is difficult to break apart due to their sticky texture. Coarser sand and compost can be added to clay soil to lighten it. The ball will disintegrate with a finger touch when the soil is sufficiently amended.

- Mulching is another crucial element. Mulch will enhance the overall condition of the soil in your garden and improve the aesthetics of your landscaping. Mulching is simple, but a few tricks help you achieve the desired aesthetic and provide the necessary cover for your plants to thrive. Shelter garden beds use a layer of mulch to prevent weed growth and reduce water usage. When the soil is adequately mulched to keep the soil surface in the dark, the germination of annual weed seeds is less likely. Even a thin layer of mulch, which acts as nature's moisture retainer, can reduce water evaporation from the soil's surface. A thicker layer of mulch can save water usage by as much as 50%.

- Compost or bark-based, dark-colored organic mulches create a tranquil, natural-looking garden. Consider using bright gravel mulch to give your yard a vivid appearance.

Straw is a great mulch for practical gardening, including vegetable gardens. Avoid using decorative bark or colored 45. Look for fine-textured mulches, such as cocoa hulls, compost, or twice-shredded bark, to get the most benefit from a thin mulch covering. Try heavier layers of coarse-textured mulches, such as bark fragments or straw, for an airy mulch. Avoid spreading grass clippings or other fine-textured mulch in dense layers that can mat down and suffocate the soil.

- Directly on the garden site, cover the newspaper with a thick layer of compost or mulch to eradicate sod or heavy weeds. Unwanted flora that receives this treatment doesn't get sunlight and gradually withers away, adding organic materials to the soil. The newspaper also disintegrates. Woody mulch, such as shredded bark, consumes nitrogen as it decomposes. Apply additional nitrogen to stop soil nitrogen plants' growth needs from being consumed by degradation.

- After planting in the autumn, mulch young plants with chopped leaves or straw to guard against winter root rot. A little mulch used soon after planting might aid in maintaining soil moisture and promote ongoing root development.

- Add a thick layer of mulch to existing gardens and let it decay. As the mulch breaks down into nutrient soup, minerals are released that seep into the soil and nurture existing plants. Humic acid, another byproduct of degradation, clumps small clay particles together to create lighter soil.

- The winter season is when mulching is most important. Frost heaving is the process of young plants being forced out of the ground due to soil alternately expanding and contracting due to freezing and thawing. When the earth begins to freeze, mulch liberally with an airy substance, such as straw, to keep the soil frozen until spring, when the mulch may be removed.

- Ground covers and evergreen perennials should be mulched with evergreen boughs in the winter to prevent winter burn, the polar opposite of sunburn. When the earth is frozen, the wind is fierce, and the sun is shining, moisture is drained from the weak leaves and is not replenished by the frozen roots. Vulnerable greenery is covered in a protective coating of evergreen boughs, probably produced by recycling Christmas tree branches. Straw will also work, particularly in colder regions with less likelihood of wintertime decay.

- If you reside in a snowy place, rejoice! You may be able to cultivate plants that won't survive the winter in snowless places farther south since snow is the greatest mulch of all. Don't let rocky ground demotivate you. With a little effort and the right soil additions, you can have a garden overflowing with your favorite flowers.

Fertilization techniques

Even though fertilizing flowers is crucial, beginners often forget to do so. Unlike granules, liquid plant food is instantly accessible for absorption and acts more quickly.

However, more frequent applications are required since it depletes considerably more quickly. But using it isn't challenging. Every time you water your beds, you may add it to your watering can, put it in a hose-end attachment, or use any handheld sprayer to administer it. You may use compost in outdoor pots or garden beds as a beautiful, natural fertilizer for flowers. It may be added to a potting mix for outdoor containers or sprinkled over the soil. Well-composted organic materials are substantially less costly than chemical products and won't burn your plants.

It doesn't matter what time you fertilize flower beds and pots; you may do it in the morning, day, or evening. Depending on the season, you should start feeding your flowers in the spring and cease in the late summer. When they are dormant in autumn and winter, avoid fertilizing them. However, before adding any fertilizer to the soil, ensure it is wet. Flowers should never be fertilized if they are anxious, thirsty, or otherwise stressed since this might seriously harm or even kill them. Very dry plants will absorb fertilizer much more quickly than adequately hydrated ones, increasing the likelihood that they may catch fire. So be sure to give your plants a healthy sip of water if they seem thirsty and let them soak it up before you feed them.

Apply slow-release granules at the planting time or in early spring for optimal results. Then repeat it two or three more times during the summer. Flowers should be fertilized with liquid fertilizers in early spring and once more every two to four weeks over the summer. To simplify it, you may give them a diluted dose every time you water them.

First and foremost, you must also realize that using too much fertilizer will hurt your plants. More is not better in this case. However, another major advantage of choosing organic goods over synthetic chemicals is that overfeeding isn't a big problem. Whether the flowers are in the ground or pots and how big your garden bed or planter is will determine the precise quantity you need.

How to Fertilize the Flower Gardens?

When using liquid plant food, gently pour the mixture around your flowers after combining the necessary water-soluble fertilizer with water. You may put it in a handheld sprayer or hose attachment to simplify applying to big garden beds. Spraying chemical compounds directly onto foliage should be avoided, particularly in the sun. This might burn the leaves and seriously harm the plant. Apply the granules uniformly over the soil's surface and all around the bases of the plants when using granular fertilizers. Don't let any pellets land on the foliage. Use a trowel or a hand rake to work them into the topsoil layer. Water the flowers well after scattering the dry pellets to let the fertilizer absorb more quickly.

CHAPTER 3: INNOVATIVE CULTIVATION METHODS

An in-depth discussion of many innovative methods that enhance the beauty of nature is provided in this topic.

Successional Planting

Wondering if succession planting is the right choice for your garden? Undoubtedly, gardening for successive harvests can add a level of complication to your garden management, and you may be asking yourself whether it is worth it.

To ensure a steady supply of crops and lengthen the harvest season, succession planting is a technique of staggered crop multiplication. You may use this technique to consistently harvest your preferred vegetables from spring through October with just a little planning and imagination! Vegetables may be harvested all year round, even in tiny spaces, with minimal preparation. To ensure a steady supply of harvestable food throughout the season, succession planting is the practice of sowing crops at intervals of 7 to 21 days. After the first crop is harvested, succession planting also entails planting a fresh crop. The second or third crop may be different or identical to the first. Succession planting is crucial for determinate crops that simultaneously produce all their fruit (or any edible material). With indeterminate cucumbers, tomatoes, melons, and peppers, the fruit will continue to be produced on the same plant; therefore, succession planting is unnecessary. Similarly, herb plants often allow for several harvests and will continue to grow. Look at the label on the seed package to determine if the tomato variety you've picked is determinate or indeterminate.

Benefits of Successional Planting

If you desire fresh vegetables throughout the entire season but lack the time or space to prepare and store a large crop, you may want to consider succession planting. Succession planting offers numerous benefits. Here are some reasons to try it:

- Do you want to make the most of your garden's space?

- Are you looking to extend your growing season as much as possible?

- Do you want to minimize the risk of bad weather, pests, or diseases affecting your crops?

- Would you like to have a continuous supply of your favorite vegetables?

- Are you interested in increasing your yields?

After harvesting a quick-growing crop, such as radishes, you can plant warm-season transplants like tomatoes or peppers. In the spring, plant greens, and you can even fit in a few plants before planting autumn crops such as broccoli in mid-summer. You can also sow certain crops, such as peas, in the spring and then plant another batch later on. Peas, cabbage, beans, and greens can be planted and harvested in both seasons. For example, plant lettuce in the spring, followed by a crop with a short growing season in the summer, such as peas, before planting lettuce again in the autumn. It's even possible to sow lettuce or kale in the autumn after a late summer crop of peppers or cucumbers.

As you might have guessed, there are several advantages to repeated seed sowing. Succession planting benefits everyone involved and, in my view, is well worth the effort! There are many options for succession planting, so feel free to experiment with different plans while keeping crop rotation in mind when making your decisions.

Cold Frames

Adding cold frames to your yard is the easiest approach to lengthening the growing season. Simple wooden boxes called 'cold frames' have an open bottom and a solid, transparent top. When the mercury drops, they focus and trap the sun's rays to create an interior microclimate more favorable to plants. You're not far off if you think this sounds like a greenhouse. Despite being smaller than greenhouses, cold frames provide some of the same advantages. Gardeners often use cold frames as a temporary solution in the spring, autumn, and winter.

Benefits of Cold Frames

According to Eliot Coleman's book "The Winter Harvest Handbook," installing a cold frame in your garden is equivalent to moving your beds 500 miles south. This is because a cold frame creates a microclimate that is 1.5 zones warmer than your current location. As a result, you can start planting seeds early in the spring. Crops may be delayed and harvested beyond the height of the growing season. However, cold frames do more than merely warm the air and soil; they shield sensitive plants from pests and frost. They are accessible to practically everyone and often portable, making purchasing or constructing them affordable.

How are cold frames put to use?

Like a greenhouse, cold frames contain and collect the sun's rays to utilize solar energy to warm the soil, air, and plants. They are not like greenhouses where you can stroll around. It's preferable to keep your cold frames as empty as possible since there will be less air inside to keep warm. Cold frames are often constructed taller at the rear and facing south to optimize the aspect. The typical cold frame has a lid that slopes gently and is set on hinges that can open and shut. It is typically between 1 and 2 feet high. Some versions are partly buried in the earth for increased insulation.

This brings up a couple of crucial cold frame laws:

- Ensure that your cold frames are always placed in a sunny area.

- Don't forget to include ventilation. This might be as simple as placing a prop under your lid on warm days.

- To optimize heat and light, keep the tops of the cold frames clear of snow and leaves.

- Avoid overwatering. Environments in cold frames are often damp because evaporation can't readily escape.

Indoor Gardening

Growing plants in one or two containers is a basic form of indoor gardening, but more complex setups can yield various fruits, herbs, vegetables, and flowers. As mentioned, it involves cultivating different fruits and vegetables that you would typically grow outdoors. This can be due to various reasons such as limited outdoor space, challenging weather conditions for growing your preferred produce, or a desire to have your herbs conveniently indoors. Whatever your motivation, indoor gardening can be a lot of fun and highly rewarding. With the right indoor setup and space, you can easily grow a variety of plants within the comfort of your home. The key is to ensure that the plants you choose are suitable for the indoor environment where you intend to grow them. There are two main methods for indoor gardening: the traditional method, where you set up your own setup, or the smart gardening kits, which handle most of the work for you.

How to Get Started with Indoor Gardening

Although it may seem intimidating at first, indoor gardening is straightforward once you get started. When growing indoors, there are a few factors to consider. Let's take a closer look at each of them individually:

• Space

Depending on your preferences, you can allocate a small or large area for an indoor garden. You can grow various types of plants on a windowsill or a table, including tomatoes. Larger growers or those more dedicated may opt to set up a dedicated table or bench for their garden. If using a table, choose a location with flooring or linoleum so that you can place a tarp beneath it to collect any inevitable water drips. Shelves, despite occupying minimal space, provide ample planting space.

When using shelves, ensure that each plant receives enough light, as this may require different grow lamps for each shelf.

• Light

Plants require light for photosynthesis and survival. Insufficient light can result in tall and spindly growth, limited leaf expansion, and a lack of blossoms or fruit. Even plants positioned near a window may not receive adequate light during the winter months to thrive.

When purchasing a grow light, there are a few things to consider:

1. Plants have photoreceptors that absorb specific light wavelengths, so regular light bulbs are ineffective.

2. The light should be positioned as close to the plant as possible without burning the leaves.

3. Most plants thrive with 14-16 hours of direct sunlight or artificial light. You can use various methods to determine if your plant is receiving enough light. Insufficient light often results in small leaves, thin stems, and lighter-than-normal foliage color.

4. The hormone "florigen" regulates flowering and budding. Long-day plants require 14-18 hours of light daily to

produce the necessary amount of florigen for blooming and growth, while short-day plants need 10-13 hours of light each day. Excessive light can disrupt florigen production in short-day plants, preventing them from flowering.

• Temperature

For most plants, a temperature range of 65-75°F (18-24°C) is ideal, with a 10°F (6°C) difference in either direction generally acceptable. Overheated plants tend to be stunted and weak, while excessively cold temperatures can lead to yellowing and leaf drop.

• Growing Medium

The soil found outdoors is unsuitable for indoor gardens as it is often too dense and may contain pests and weed seeds. Indoor gardens benefit from a proper planting medium. Look for a blend specifically designed for indoor plants. A good growth medium should be porous, allowing for excellent drainage, and have enough organic matter to retain moisture and nutrients. Most commercially available organic mixtures will work, or you can create your own.

• Selecting Plants

Almost any plant can be grown indoors as long as it doesn't

grow too large. However, it's important to consider growing plants that have similar water requirements, humidity needs, and light preferences.

Here are some popular options for an indoor garden: Pansy, Geranium, Zinnia, Roses, Alyssum, Candytuft, Marigold, Begonia, Petunia, and Shasta Daisy.

CHAPTER 4: EXTENDING THE FLOWERING PERIOD THROUGH MICROCLIMATE

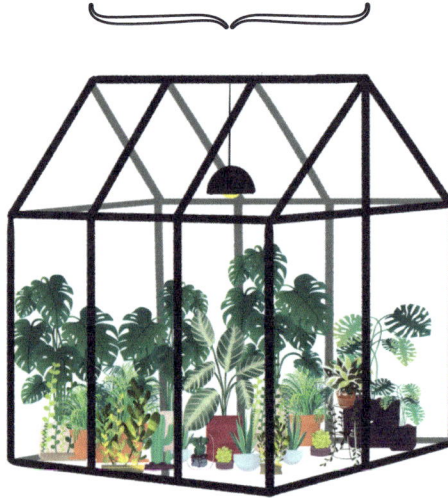

Microclimate refers to the climatic conditions within a relatively small area, typically a few meters above and below the Earth's surface. This includes areas beneath plant canopies as well as the surfaces of oceans and other bodies of water. It is often used to describe the conditions on the surfaces of glaciers and terrestrial ecosystems. Above and below the Earth's surface, temperature and humidity gradients are most pronounced. While individual species may only tolerate a narrow range of climates, the complexity of microclimates is essential for supporting a wide range of flora and fauna, as they create unique environments that allow different species to coexist and interact.

Temperature, wind, humidity, turbulence, dew, heat balance, frost, and evaporation are some variables that affect microclimate. The type of soil has a significant impact on microclimates. Examples of soils prone to low minimum and high maximum surface temperatures include sandy, coarse, loose, and dry soils. The surface reflection properties of soils also play a significant role; lighter-colored soils reflect more light and react less to daily heating. The capacity of the soil to absorb and hold moisture, influenced by the soil's composition and usage, is another aspect of the microclimate.

Additionally, vegetation is essential because it regulates the flow of water vapor into the atmosphere through transpiration. Plants can also reduce temperature fluctuations and insulate the soil below. Exposed areas of soil experience the greatest temperature variation. The urban heat island effect, characterized by the retention of heat in pavement and concrete during summer, creates favorable conditions for specific plant species to thrive. It also provides an opportunity to cultivate plants that would not typically thrive in this environment.While microclimates may provide the ideal conditions for certain plants, they can also create unfavorable circumstances for other plants. For example, if your yard is located in a low spot in the neighborhood, chilly air will naturally flow in, increasing the risk of late-season frost and requiring the use of hardier plant varieties. The key is to be aware of the various environmental factors in your landscape and choose plants that will thrive there.

Although long-term observation is the best method to understand these microclimates, there are several quick fixes that can help you identify the distinct characteristics of your growing area and adjust it to suit your gardening goals:

1. Survey your neighborhood for indicator plants. Despite being commonly planted in an area, certain plants are known to be "hit or miss" for gardeners. For instance, the popular Minneapolis plant known as Japanese forest grass (Hakonechloa sp.) sometimes struggles in open areas. Even though it is only considered hardy to zone 5, finding it in the neighborhood may indicate a warmer microclimate.

2. Pay attention to differences in spring bloom time, even if it's just a few days. Plants develop and bloom based on the accumulation of heat, or "heat units," rather than the passage of time. If the first peonies or other spring flowers bloom early in your microclimate, you may accumulate more "heat units"

and struggle to grow delicate perennials. On the other hand, if you have the last spring-blooming flowers relative to the region, indicating a colder microclimate, you may want to modify your garden designs to include highly hardy plants that benefit from the cooler conditions.

3. When choosing a planting location, consider heat exposure in addition to light. The success or failure of a plant depends on which side of a hill, house, or fence it is planted. Sensitive plants should be placed from south to east to west to north, in order of "hottest" to "coolest" exposure. The moderating effect of a colder north-facing garden can be advantageous for plants susceptible to early bud break or if you are cultivating a plant that thrives better in zone 3. This is why many historic farmsteads would grow vegetables that required warmer soil early in the season on south-facing slopes and apples on north-facing slopes (to avoid early bud break). Site selection should reflect plant hardiness!

4. Include "heat sinks" to expand your range in chilly locations. You can create your own microclimate, so yes! This can be as elaborate as a masonry wall or as simple as surrounding

delicate plants with dark-colored bricks to absorb and radiate heat to the plants in the early season. Even a small water feature can help mitigate abrupt temperature swings. Keep in mind that "heat sinks" made of water or stone can amplify a site's natural tendency to heat; with a southern exposure, they will intensify the heat, and in a northern location, they will remain cool longer, slowing down the warming of the surrounding garden beds.

5. Always be open to trying something new. As an old saying goes, you have to "grow it to know it" – gardening is a participatory activity. Just because a certain plant is not common in your area doesn't mean it can't thrive there. Seeing a new plant unexpectedly flourish is one of the most delightful experiences in gardening. The best gardeners learn to incorporate both the "tried and true" and the unexpected into their landscapes. If something doesn't work out the first time, try again, have fun, and remember that there's always another season to look forward to.

Power of Greenhouse

Most knowledgeable gardeners like the thought of owning a greenhouse. They consider it to be the best! They can choose what to plant, how to plant it, and what rewards will result from the labor they put in with such a place. The advantages of owning and using a greenhouse may be unclear to a beginner gardener compared to an experienced one. They may have never used one, let alone been in one. Such a place has many advantages. For you, we have selected a few. Get ready to work with your hands in the soil as you begin your quest to become the finest gardener there is.

• Environment Under Control

Your greenhouse is in your hands. You, who manage the area, decide on the amount of light, the temperature, the humidity levels in the air, the types of soil, and the plants you have.

• Protected Environment

For plants, a greenhouse is a sanctuary of safety. It lessens the likelihood of insects and other creatures harming or devouring your plants. Extreme weather events like heavy rain and droughts are less likely to occur in this greenhouse climate. It is the ideal habitat for diverse plants, from the delicate to the robust.

- Stronger Plants

You can anticipate better plants and food since you have more control over the environment. The ideal conditions you choose should be based on the specific requirements of each plant you have. You can create the ideal growth conditions for your plants by combining the aforementioned factors with protection from extremes. In our opinion, that's similar to a couple of thumbs up!

- Unlimited Gardening Seasons

You can choose the best temperature for your plants in a greenhouse since it is a controlled environment. You will then have the authority to choose the appropriate time for planting, reaping, and sowing in accordance with the season and the type of product.

- Multipurpose Setting

Using various soil types depending on the area's plants is a lovely aspect of having a greenhouse. Furthermore, greenhouses are usually multifunctional in supporting many plant species. Fruits, ornamentals, vegetables, herbs, and spices are all options in certain circumstances. Imagine if you built your greenhouse on the appropriate foundation, you could cut down on farmer market excursions. A greenhouse can be utilized to store your gardening supplies and equipment and manage the different soil types. It serves as a one-stop shop for honing your green thumb.

CHAPTER 5: UNVEILING UNIQUE FLOWER VARIETIES

Choosing the ideal flowers for your house or yard can be difficult. You must consider various factors besides seasonality, including color, climate, surroundings, sunshine, and more. This topic teaches you how to decorate your garden with beautiful flower varieties.

• Bird of Paradise (Strelitzia reginae)

Not only are the bird of paradise blooms bicolor, but they also have a distinctive form. The flower of the plant bears some resemblance to the same-named bird species, which is how the plant got its name. This tropical plant is native to South Africa and thrives in hot, muggy environments. The only options available to northern gardeners are cultivating it as an annual or overwintering it inside.

• Blue Poppy (Meconopsis betonicifolia)

The unusual blue poppy blossoms have a fuzzy yellow core and resemble blue umbrellas. These striking flowers, which can measure 4 to 5 inches across, bloom throughout the summer. Growing this plant can be a little unpredictable. It prefers a steady supply of moisture—but not an excessive amount. Additionally, it dislikes very chilly or overly hot summers or winters.

• Crown Imperial (Fritillaria imperialis)

The spring bulb plant known as Crown Imperial can grow very tall. Don't let the fact that the flowers have a smell turn you off from them. Their clusters of bell-shaped flowers create a "crown" atop the plant, making them highly distinctive and lovely. Trim the leaves to the ground after the plant becomes dormant in the summer, and mulch it to protect it from the cold.

- Secret Lust Coneflower (Echinacea 'Secret Lust')

Contrary to its popular name, Secret Lust is not a coneflower. It has a puffy center disk instead of a cone in the middle of the flower. The blooms are highly fragrant and range from one to three inches. Once they start to produce seeds, they also attract birds. It can withstand most situations except damp soil, so choose a location with sufficient drainage for this plant.

- Purple Pitcher Plant (Sarracenia purpurea)

The purple pitcher plant is a somewhat unusual species that thrives in the vicinity of ponds. It is a carnivorous plant that catches insects in its pitcher-shaped leaves, much like the more well-known Venus flytrap. Its blossoms begin as a compact ball that gradually unfolds into an intriguing form. Because this plant prefers muddy soil, maintain a consistent moisture level throughout the soil.

- Sundew (Drosera capensis)

Another unusual carnivorous plant is the sundew. The name-giving dewdrops that glitter on its small stalks fool insects into believing its fake blooms are genuine; they appear to them as drops of nectar. However, the insects become stuck in the sticky droplets as they fall on them. Sundew enjoys mucky environments, much like the purple pitcher plant. Therefore, it is essential to regularly maintain soil moisture.

• Batik Iris (Iris germanica 'Batik')

Some of the strongest, most beautiful, and fragrant blooms in the plant kingdom can be found in the iris genus. This trio of characteristics would be enough to distinguish them as special blooms even if they had no other advantages. However, the Iris germanica 'Batik' variety makes the deal more enticing by producing bicolored blooms with erratic purple and white blotches and streaks. This plant tends to grow in clusters. To keep clumps healthy and bursting with flowers, divide them every few years.

• Red Hot Poker Plant (Kniphofia spp.)

The cylindrical form of these plants and the intense hues of their long, thin flower spikes give them their name. Even some cultivars have bicolored blooms that resemble flames.

The spent flowers on this plant should be removed or deadheaded.

This will support the growth of new flowers.

• Snake Lily (Amorphophallus konjac)

Snake lilies sprout from corms that are sometimes cooked and used as food, most notably in China and Japan. Every year in the spring, each corm produces one enormous leaf and one blooming stalk. The bloom emits an unappealing rotten-smelling odor that attracts flies and other pollinators; however, after pollination, the odor disappears. Throughout the growing season, keep the soil wet but not waterlogged, and then reduce watering to prepare for winter dormancy.

• Amethyst in Snow (Centaurea montana 'Amethyst in Snow')

During spring and summer, Amethyst in Snow offers a wide variety of fascinating blooms. The exquisite bicolored flowers have a purple core surrounded by white petals. This plant's tendency to spread makes it perfect for use as a ground cover. It may be divided every few years to prevent it from spreading and to encourage new, healthy growth.

Incorporating Wild and Native Flowers into The Garden

Are you considering developing a wildflower garden but unsure of the species you ought to choose? Picking the best flower types might be a bit difficult since there are so many different kinds of wildflowers to select from! I have compiled a thorough list of the best varieties in this topic.

• Black-Eyed Susan

To prevent the plants from expanding, Black-Eyed Susan should be placed in full sunlight. Rudbeckia hirta is its scientific name. The Black-Eyed Susan won't let you down if you're a fan of the color yellow. Because it can self-seed, the plants will quickly fill your garden. Up to 3 years may pass before the Black-Eyed Susan reaches its peak height. Light is necessary for this wildflower to flourish. However, if the majority of your flowers are not exposed to direct sunshine, they may also tolerate some partial shadow. Black-Eyed Susan may grow in any soil with a modest quantity of nutrients, regardless of the kind. Black-Eyed Susans don't need much upkeep, but watering them throughout the first growing season is crucial. They may establish themselves in a healthy environment as a result.

• Blazing Star

Summer is when Blazing Star blooms, and unlike other flowers, Liatris opens its blossoms from the top of the inflorescence rather than the bottom. Liatris spicata is its scientific name. Blazing star wildflowers are so beautiful that you will only fall in love with them for that. The blazing star features white, pinkish-red, or purple-pink blooms, depending on the type you discover. The fact that this perennial flower blooms from top to bottom is an intriguing feature. The brilliant star prospers well in the sunlight. Its bushes should thus be planted in a warm, sunny location. As you prepare the soil, ensure it's not too acidic and should be moist. During the first several weeks, keep the blazing star well-watered to encourage strong root growth. But its bushes can't stand standing water. Therefore, maintaining proper drainage in the garden space is crucial. Blazing stars can endure a wide range of soil types and unfavorable soil conditions as long as the soil is sufficiently drained.

- Blanket Flower

Depending on your environment, the blanket flower may be grown as an annual or a perennial. Gaillardia sp. is the name of the species. Another simple perennial to plant in your yard is the blanket flower, which resembles a daisy. The plant expands by forming a spreading mound that covers a certain region, just as its name suggests. They sprout sooner than other perennials you choose from this list since they grow quickly, so don't be startled by that.

Red and yellow, both vibrant hues, can make any garden seem cheerful. When you are relaxing in your yard, you will, without a doubt, appreciate their vibrant, lovely company. The blanket flowers will be effective if you want to attract birds. Because they are pollinator-friendly, you will have many butterflies and bees visiting you. The perennial blanket flower adores the sun, so be sure to put it where there is plenty of exposure.

- Columbine

The columbine plant thrives in sunny environments. The ornamental impact of lovely foliage lasts the whole growing season. Aquilegia Canadensis is the name of the species. The fact that columbines self-seed is one feature you'll adore. All you have to do after planting them is relax and wait for them to blossom. They are resilient and can adapt to a wide range of climatic and soil conditions. The greatest locations to cultivate columbines are in areas with some shade. However, this does not imply that your wildflowers won't thrive in direct sunlight. Columbines may grow well in the sun with periodic watering. The columbines' growing blossoms come in a variety of hues, from orange, vivid blue, and red to even pink and yellow. Your garden should have a lovely and enduring glow in the spring and summer, thanks to these hues.

• California Poppy

The orange poppy is a typical annual flower endemic to North America. Eschscholzia californica is its official scientific name. The greatest perennials to acclimate your surroundings to nature are California poppies. They have cup-shaped blooms that fill any garden area with a blaze of summer color. These lovely flowers often manifest themselves as vivid orange or yellow blossoms.

This annual wildflower can thrive in various hardiness zones and is widespread across North America. It may readily be found in various wildflower mixes that can be bought at nearby retailers. Blooms typically occur from March to May and have a shorter lifespan.

• Dutchman's Breeches

Dutchman's Breeches have white and yellow flowers or pale pink; peduncles are almost straight. The name of the species is Dicentra Cucullaria. Who doesn't like listening to bumblebees singing in the garden? We all do as garden enthusiasts. The Dutchman's breeches are a fantastic choice since they blossom early and not simply because bumblebees are attracted to them. In addition to relying on bees for pollination, you may care for these blossoms by ensuring adequate litter on the ground. Breeches do great in the shadows. You will have plenty of time to accomplish other things thanks to their little upkeep.

Exotic Species for Year-Round Blooming

• **Rose**

Roses have a broad range of color tones and produce fragrant blossoms. The growth conditions are favorable in India, and cultivars like Kashmiri Rose and Desi Rose bloom year-round.

• **Lantana**

It is an evergreen tropical shrub that produces clusters of white, orange, yellow, pink, and red flowers. This plant does well in warm areas and prefers well-draining soil.

• **Adenium**

Adenium, sometimes called desert rose, is a magnificent blooming plant perfect for bonsai gardens. For year-round blossoms, you can plant them both inside and outside in plastic containers.

• **Bougainvillea**

Growing bougainvilleas in your yard can provide a flowery feast all year. They can be grown as a ground cover, in pots, or on trellises. They require little maintenance and can withstand drought.

• Hibiscus

The Hibiscus plant, often called rose mallow, is well-known for its beautiful, vibrant yellow, white, and red blooms. By blooming all year long, it adds beauty to your garden.

• Ixora

Its botanical name is Ixora coccinea, and its Indian name is Rugmini. Ixora grows readily and requires no further care or maintenance. It comes in lovely red, yellow, and vibrant orange hues. The name of a Hindu god is the source of Rugmini's Indian name.

• Crossandra

Its botanical name is Crossandra infundibuliform, and its Indian name is Priyadarsha. Crossandras are magnificent perennial blooms that thrive in loamy, rich soil with good drainage.

This plant is also known as the "firecracker flower" because it produces orange and red flowers. They can also be grown indoors.

- **Kalanchoes**

Its botanical name is Kalanchoe blossfeldiana, and its Indian name is Flaming Katy. Beautiful succulent plants called kalanchoes have charming little blooms and flat, green leaves. They can be planted indoors and outdoors, giving your yard a splash of color.

- **Christ Plant**

Its botanical name is Euphorbia milii, and its Indian name is Millii. This plant, native to Madagascar, is also called the Christ thorn and the crown of thorns. It is a perennial shrub with beautiful little green blooms and green leaves that you can enjoy all year long!

- **Tibouchina**

Its botanical name is Tibouchina urvilleana, and its Indian name is Begum Bahar. This plant, often called the Princess Flower, has gorgeous purple, brilliant blooms and glossy, green foliage. It can reach a height of 10 to 15 feet and has many summer flowers.

• Jasmine

Its botanical name is Jasminum, and its Indian name is Chameli. Grow jasmine to give your yard its captivating scent. It is a perennial evergreen plant with well-known medicinal qualities. If you want the plant to become bushy, you can pinch off the growing tips.

• Golden Trumpet

Its botanical name is Allamanda cathartica, and its Indian name is Pilaghanti. This lovely blooming plant, native to South America and Brazil, has green foliage and yellow trumpet-shaped blooms. Additionally, it releases a milky sap that is hazardous, so keep your children and dogs away.

• Butterfly Pea

Its botanical name is Clitoria ternatea, and its Indian name is Aparajita. The Butterfly Pea's incredibly·gorgeous plant has large, cobalt blue and white blossoms. It is important in India, where Hindus frequently present Lord Shiva with this flower.

- **Begonia**

Its botanical name is Begonia x semperflorens-cultorum, and its Indian name is Common Begonia. Begonias are beautiful plants with delicate but vibrant white and pink blooms. They can be displayed beautifully in both outdoor flower beds and containers.

- **Verbena**

Its botanical name is Verbena hybrida, and its Indian name is Barbara. Verbena is one of the nicest flowers that bloom all year. It has rose, lavender, purple, blue, pink, and white flowers. The height of this blooming plant can reach 4-6 feet.

CHAPTER: 6: DESIGNING FOR CONTINUOUS BLOOMS

Imagine a beautiful flower garden that is awash in color from the earliest signs of spring through the first frost in the fall. You must visit the garden center in the spring with one idea: to get year-round color in your flower beds, you need a continuous run of bloom. It is insufficient to only choose plants that bloom beautifully in the late spring.

Although flowers may seem beautiful at the moment, you must consider the times when they won't be in bloom.

What will replace them as a source of color? The trick for new gardeners is to become aware of these options, as some plants fortunately bloom both before and after them. Foliage plants might also fill the gaps.

Designing for Year-Round Blooms.

You must include some evergreens to keep your yard visually interesting throughout the year. Indeed, if you want color throughout the year, planting trees and bushes is a terrific idea. In addition to their blooms, they have interesting shapes and foliage. Perennial flowers are essential for any gardener wanting vibrant color, so let's explore some excellent options to design your year-round garden. Both novice and experienced gardeners will find everything they want in this flower garden design.

Snowdrops: Early-Spring Bloomers

It's a lovely time of year in early spring. Bulb plants are among the first to bloom and welcome us during this time. Many of them are presumably already known to you, and you likely appreciate them for their propensity for early blossoming. One of the first flowers to bloom is the snowdrop (Galanthus nivalis), although Crocus will follow soon after. Two bigger spring-flowering bulbs comparable to G. nivalis that you may cultivate for more impact are:

1. 6–12-inch giant snowdrops (G. elwesii)

2. A one-foot-tall spring snowflake (Leucojum vernum)

- **Adonis**

When the winter snow melts, bulb plants are a great idea, but consider other options to add even more color to your flower beds. Adonis Vernalis, think of that hunk with the yellow petals. It is a perennial herbaceous plant, not a bulb. It resembles the bulb plant winter aconite (Eranthis hyemalis) in terms of appearance and flowering time.

- **Dutchman's Breeches**

Growing bulb plants has the disadvantage that their leaves remain in your flower garden after their flowers have faded and fallen off. Furthermore, you shouldn't remove the leaves until they have turned brown since, while they are still green, they provide much-needed nutrients to the bulbs. Here is the issue: These leaves, which are now unattractive, are a blight on your landscape.

These plants are categorized as "spring ephemerals" because they are transient. In April, they produce their distinctive floral display before disappearing. There is no need for gangly foliage to remain unattended and clutter up the flower bed. Bleeding hearts (Dicentra spectabilis), which provide a more well-known option for landscaping in mid-spring, are linked to Dutchman's breeches.

- **Peony**

The value traditionally cultivated peonies (Paeonia lactiflora) provide to your flower beds in May is well known to most gardeners. However, if you're searching for something fresh, think about "tree peonies" (P. suffruticosa). They are not trees. Despite being referred to as "sub-shrubs," they serve the same purpose as perennials in flower gardens. You can count on vibrant flowers that are big enough to draw attention whether you plant P. lactiflora or P. suffruticosa.

- **Torch Lily**

In many places, the temperature heats up significantly in June. The flowerbed also blooms at that time because torch lilies (Kniphofia; sometimes known as "red hot poker plants") do. They flower in various hues, including the mango-orange shade of

Terra Nova Nursery's Mango Popsicle (yellow, orange, red, etc.). They provide color to your landscape into the late summer since they are perennials with lengthy bloom cycles. A torch lily's bloom stalk is made up of several tiny blossoms. The ones near the base of the stalk open first. They change color as they ascend, but the top of the stem retains its brilliant color. The result is often two-toned (for instance, orange at the top and yellowish at the bottom). Another reddish-orange option that sticks with the orange theme for early summer is Firebird coneflower.

- **Mid-Summer Star**

July is the month of lilies. If not Lilium Stargazer specifically, at least give one of the other varieties a try. Although some may consider them "common," the benefits they bring remain as substantial as ever. One of them is their delightful fragrance. Despite their popular name, Easter lilies (Lilium longiflorum) bloom in the Northeastern United States during this time if you cultivate them in your landscape rather than using greenhouse stock.

- **Garden Phlox**

Some tried-and-true flower varieties, such as garden phlox or "tall" phlox (Phlox paniculata), take over the floral throne in late summer. An interesting variety is Nora Leigh, which has bicolored blooms and variegated foliage. Another traditional plant that offers plenty of color for late summer landscaping is the Black-eyed Susan. In addition to having long-lasting flowers, this perennial also tolerates drought, which is helpful in the sweltering heat of August.

- **Montauk Daisy**

Even if you live in a frigid area, autumn need not signify a "fall from grace" when it comes to color in your flower beds. Consider the Montauk daisy (Nipponanthemum nipponicum) to keep the flower color deep into the fall. Cut back the Montauk daisy, also known as the "Nippon daisy," in early summer to prepare it for autumn flowering. Pruning it keeps it smaller, which enhances the autumn show.

- **Rose**

Let's look at three shrubs that add color to your perennial flowers, starting with Candy Oh! Roses. Shrubs are like the "bones" of a landscape. By growing a variety of shrubs in your garden, from those that bloom in early spring to those that do so in late summer, you can ensure that you will have something beautiful to look at throughout the summer and spring. While many shrubs are valued more for their autumn leaf color than their flowers, they provide blooms to your flower gardens. Landscape roses require little maintenance, but that isn't their only advantage. They bloom well into fall, making them great for adding color throughout the year. You don't have to be afraid to trim them aggressively to keep them small in your flower beds since they don't mind pruning.

- **Winter Heath**

If you reside in the North, the phrase "flowers for winter" may seem absurd unless we discuss indoor landscaping. However, there is one exception: winter heath (Erica x darleyensis). This heather-related plant may start flowering in November and last all the way through the colder months of December, January, and February, and even into the first days of spring. Winter heath may have small blooms, but what they lack in size, they more than make up for in quantity. Moreover, any flower that blooms outdoors in a cold location throughout the winter is valued, regardless of size. Winter heath is a small shrub that can be grown in your flower garden like a perennial due to its diminutive size.

- **Jasmine**

Winter jasmine (Jasminum nudiflorum) is one of several varieties of this flower. If you reside in the North, grow it in a protected area, and it will reward you with flowers in February. We started with plants that bloom in March (snowdrops and Adonis), so that completes the cycle. Winter jasmine is a type of plant that grows on vines. Shearing is a simple way to keep it small. Depending on how you prune it, it can either look like a shrub or a vine.

How to Design Flower Beds and Borders

Always see gardens as very individual pieces of art. Like all art forms, taste will be highly subjective, with each individual having a unique idea of beauty. It's crucial, in my opinion, to comprehend fundamental design concepts for two reasons. Firstly, you can break the rules in a smart manner if you are aware of them. Secondly, it gives you some assurance that the design you come up with won't be a total failure. But ultimately, the only thing that counts is that you like your garden; your judgment is the most significant. In addition to formal and informal gardens, there are two main types of garden beds: island beds and borders.

Since the surroundings will help define the size of the new bed, I find these beds easier to visualize than island beds, at least for me. A backdrop anchors a border. It can be a house, a row of hedges, a fence, or anything else that provides a somewhat substantial background. Borders are only visible from one side. A floral border is often long and thin, but this isn't always the case. The required depth of your bed will partly depend on its length. The dimensions of the bed are crucial. A short bed does not need to be as deep; a bed that is 3 feet by 8 feet can work just fine. If possible, a longer bed will require additional depth. A bed that is 12 feet by 100 feet will appear proportionate. Most residential gardens typically feature beds that are between five and fifty feet long. In this case, the recommended depth should be between three and six to eight feet. Access to the inside of any bed deeper than four feet is necessary for weeding and other maintenance needs (you can only reach so far). Access is often provided by paths or stepping stones. Some ground rules include:

- The bed is 16 feet by 6 feet, and the garden needs at least six hours of sunshine daily. Each of the 13 plant varieties is mass-planted for maximum color and immediate curb appeal. You can use the design as a boundary or an island to your advantage.

- To make larger beds, increase the number of plants by two or three.

- If you're short on time or space, shorten the bed to 8 feet, reduce the number of plants, and exclude the large "Black Lace" elderberry bush.

- To create a focal point in the center of a lawn, start with an elderberry and taller perennials, then surround them with shorter-stemmed plants. Place the Rozanne geranium and 'Obsidian' heuchera near the bed's border.

Tips for Every Season's Success

- Place the potted plants on the bed to understand how the garden will appear before you begin digging. Don't forget to provide room between the plants so they can spread out.

- Plant the bed from the rear to the front. For a lush appearance, plant tulip bulbs densely (approximately 5 per square foot of bed).

- Set perennials and shrubs at the same depth as they are in pots. Remove the dead flowers after they bloom to allow the bulbs to focus their efforts on conserving nutrients for the next season rather than producing seeds. Once they turn brown, remove the tulip leaves. The neighboring perennials will hide the wilting leaves, so don't worry about aesthetics.

- Fertilize your plants if you want them to grow well. Remove mulch from each plant's base early in the spring and cover it with an inch of compost. Incorporate slow-release fertilizer or bonemeal sparingly into the top layer of soil over the bulbs in July. (Note: Bonemeal can attract mice that will rummage around your yard for bones.) Find out more about organic soil improvements.

- Cover the bed with 3 inches of mulch. It will aid in moisture retention and weed suppression. Use an organic ingredient like leaf mold or chopped-up bark, which decomposes and releases nutrients into the soil. Mulch made of cedar bark is also a great option because the resins prevent fungal diseases and discourage insects from breeding. Find out more about mulch.

- Remove wilting flowers to promote more blooms on perennials. If conditions are favorable, shrubs will bloom again after shedding their old blossoms.

- Wait until the first signs of fresh green growth in early spring to remove brown leaves from perennials. Dead debris protects plant roots from severe winter temperatures.

- If pruning is necessary, wait until after the shrubs have bloomed rather than doing it in early spring.

- Be patient after planting your three-season plot. By the second season, perennials will have grown to their full size and beauty. Shrubs develop more slowly and may take three to five years after planting to reach their full size.

How to Incorporate Perennials and Annuals into Your Garden?

Obtaining color in the yard all season long is one of the most challenging tasks for a gardener. Some of us find it easy to create a vibrant, blooming spring garden, but when the midsummer heat arrives, our gardens often fade into a sea of green—and even brown. Fortunately, there are a few gardening methods to keep your yard looking magazine-worthy throughout the year, and some of them are surprisingly simple. Creating a beautiful garden takes time! Just like your home decor, your garden isn't planned in a single season. It requires patience, time, and attention to detail to ensure that you create a long-lasting and continuously blooming landscape. Keep a gardening notebook and record the times of the year when new annual and perennial flower pairings can be introduced, as well as their blooming periods. With the passage of time and the valuable insights provided in this guide, you will discover effective tips and solutions to create a magnificent, magazine-worthy garden that reflects your desires.

- As the seasons change, it's beneficial to visit your local garden center.

Throughout the year, garden centers stock new items to align with the changing seasons, just like any other retailer. When the vibrant spring blooms begin to fade, you'll find a display of summer perennials and annuals that thrive in the heat. By staying aware of the requirements for each season, you can cultivate your plants accordingly. Take the opportunity to explore what's currently blooming and available at your nearest garden center.

- Extend the Bloom Times

As the blossoms start to fade, we often assume that the plant is done, but that's not the case! Many perennials and annuals can bloom again under the right conditions. Deadheading, fertilizing, watering, or even relocating a potted container to a sunnier spot can give your plant a wake-up call, encouraging it to redirect more energy into producing new flowers.

- Mix and match the annuals and perennials.

The idea is to have an always-blooming garden, but adding some annuals when the summer heat starts to cause our perennial plants to go from bloom to disaster isn't cheating. Adding some annuals can help fill the gaps, even though many combinations of perennial flowers allow your garden to bloom at every window of the growing season. Additionally, annuals allow you to express your inner creative gardener and often change the appearance of your garden.

- Invest in perennials and annuals that will rebloom.

  We've previously discussed how deadheading, fertilizing,

and providing our garden plants with enough light and water can encourage them to produce new flowers. There are also several types that promise us a spectacular garden from autumn to spring. These are known as rebloomers or perpetual bloomers. Here are a few species to keep an eye out for; plant these mixtures of annual and perennial flowers to make the garden shine from the spring equinox until the time when pumpkins are harvested in the autumn! Annuals that love to bloom throughout the year include Salvia, Geranium, Petunia, and Begonia. Perennials that love to bloom throughout the year include Endless Summer Hydrangea, Dianthus, and Shrub Roses.

CHAPTER 7 HOW TO NURTURE AND CARE FOR YOUR YEAR-ROUND BLOOMING GARDEN

Your fruits, plants, and vegetables will grow better and last longer if you take good care of your garden. Nearly all plants need a few hours of direct sunlight, although various species have varying needs. Understanding how to properly care for your garden is crucial if you want your lovely flowers and outdoor vegetables to last the seasons.

Essential Watering Techniques and Irrigation System

Anyone can water a plant. However, understanding how plants utilize water and considering other factors requires time and expertise. Some examples include the type of plant, its size, the soil's texture, the recent weather conditions, solar exposure, the time of day, and the season. Caring for the garden shouldn't be a routine chore. You must pay attention since a plant's water needs are always changing.

Watering techniques

Most gardens seldom use proper watering techniques. They either provide too little or too much water during irrigation. The person who underwater their plants often isn't aware of how long it takes to properly water an area; instead, they sprinkle lightly every day. In fact, daily light misting of plants is harmful. The soil is regularly lightly dampened to a depth of less than an inch, while the roots of most plants extend much deeper. Light misting does nothing to alleviate drought stress experienced by plants growing in hot, dry soil; it only settles the dust.

- Instead of giving a little water daily, give plants a good soaking once a week. Water the soil until it is moist to a depth of five to six inches. With this type of irrigation, water can reach the soil's surface, where roots can easily absorb it. A well-soaked soil retains moisture for many days, while soil that receives only an inch or two of rainfall dries up in a day.

- On the other hand, some people water their plants too often and excessively, drowning them. The signs of overwatering or underwatering are the same. The top and edges of the leaves turn brown, eventually spreading throughout the plant and causing the leaves to fall off. These symptoms occur because there is either too much or too little water in the plant tissue.

- Soil with excess water becomes oxygen-deficient, which harms the root system. Plant roots need oxygen to survive, but when the soil is excessively wet, there isn't enough oxygen available. In such cases, roots stop absorbing water and eventually die. Then, the leaves start showing signs of water deficiency. Many times, gardeners apply additional water after observing these signs of dehydration, exacerbating the condition and often leading to the plant's rapid demise.

- Thoroughly saturate the soil during each watering, then wait for a while to allow the plants to absorb most of the water before watering again.

Irrigating Methods

Flooding, Sprinkling, furrow irrigation, and drip irrigation are the four different types of irrigation. Before choosing the 'right' system, take into account the tools and techniques used in each approach.

Choose a system that will provide enough moisture for plants without wasting water.

- Hose-end Sprinkling

The most well-liked and typical watering technique is sprinkler irrigation, often called 'hose-end overhead sprinkling.' Sprinkler units can be quickly set up and relocated. They are cheap to acquire, but if used improperly, they can waste a lot of water. Sprinkler equipment can cost as little as a few dollars for a small fixed device to as much as $50 for self-propelled ones. Although not required, a solid-set sprinkler system for a small garden might cost more than $100. The best investment is an impact-driving sprinkler that can be configured to water a complete or half circle. Sprinkler irrigation offers certain benefits. The method can be used on both flat and sloping surfaces.

Water percolates downhill from the surface, bringing salts with it, preventing salt accumulation. Different plantings may receive varying amounts of water to meet the needs of the plants. However, there are certain disadvantages. Use sprinkler watering in the morning to give the soil surface time to dry before dusk. Water distribution becomes uneven when rinsing in wind speeds exceeding 5 mph. If your water is of low quality, the mist dries on the leaves and may leave enough salt behind to harm them. Strong gusts can carry the water to the yards of neighbors. Attempting to cover a rectangular or square space with a circular pattern also wastes some water. If the garden is larger than the sprinkler pattern, move the sprinkler unit regularly. When using caged tomatoes or trellised crops, set the sprinkler on a stand so the spray will arch up and over the leaf canopy. Working at the wrong time, in windy conditions, or at night can harm plants and pollute water.

- Flood Irrigation

One of the earliest types of irrigation is flooding. It is often employed in regions with intense summer heat, particularly in big agricultural operations. It can also be used in backyard gardens. First, a small dam surrounds the area that needs to be watered. Then, the soil is exposed to water until the dammed region is submerged. Only level ground and soil with adequate clay content that allows the water to spread out over the surface and seep in slowly and evenly can benefit from flooding. The soil should not remain submerged under water for more than a few hours.

While flood irrigation has advantages in removing excessive soluble salts from the soil through leaching, it can have certain disadvantages. It may result in water wastage as it is easy to apply more water than necessary to meet the typical plant requirements. Controlling runoff can be challenging. Additionally, flooded soil can have a low oxygen level, causing damage to fast-developing plants due to oxygen deprivation. Fruits that come into contact with flooded soil often remain damp and tend to decay.

- Furrow Irrigation

Water application via furrows is a common practice, especially in vegetable gardens. Soil with suitable clay is necessary for effective furrow irrigation, so water gradually runs over the shallow ditches between the furrows and rows. Before much of the water has been absorbed into the top end of the rows, it must first reach the lower end. In many open or sandy soils, water seeps in too rapidly and never reaches the end of the row because the soil is so porous. To address this issue in gardens with sandy soil, use shorter rows. The furrow technique makes it simple to water most gardens by creating shallow ditches using a hoe or shovel. Make a single, shallow ditch that extends from end to end to test furrow irrigation. It's okay if the water moves 20 to 30 feet in a short period of time. If the water drains too quickly at the upper end, divide the garden lengthwise into two or more runs and irrigate each run individually. In small gardens on flat land, use a winding ditch to direct water up and down short rows. The amount of water available and your imagination will determine how many rows can be watered simultaneously. Furrow irrigation ensures that the leaves and fruit of upright plants like peppers and beans remain dry. For newly planted seedlings, you can irrigate as frequently as necessary with running water to keep the seedbed moist. Unlike spray watering, furrow irrigation results in less surface soil compaction and crusting in raised beds. The only tools required to transfer water from the home tap to the garden are a shovel or hoe and a length of hose. However, furrow irrigation does have significant drawbacks. Mulching over the furrows to preserve them can be difficult, if not impossible. It can be a challenging task to train vining plants away from the furrows. In locations with saline water, salts can build up in the middle of a row and harm plants. If there isn't sufficient water, water a few rows at a time before switching to another group. This process can be time-consuming, and water waste at the ends of the rows is a common issue.

- Drip Irrigation

Drip irrigation is an efficient and highly effective technique for watering plants that surpasses traditional methods. This approach involves the precise delivery of water directly to the plant's root zone through a network of tubes or hoses equipped with small emitters or drippers.

Unlike other watering methods, drip irrigation ensures a slow and steady release of small amounts of water directly to the plant's root zone. This targeted approach allows plants to efficiently absorb water, minimizing the risks of evaporation and runoff. One of the most notable advantages of drip irrigation is its significant contribution to water conservation. By providing a focused water supply to each plant, drip irrigation greatly reduces water loss through evaporation and runoff. This method has the potential to save up to 50% of water compared to traditional watering techniques. Not only does this benefit the environment, but it also supports water conservation efforts and can lead to long-term cost savings.

In addition to its water-saving benefits, drip irrigation promotes healthier plant growth by ensuring water is delivered directly to the roots. This precise watering system helps prevent the issues of overwatering or underwatering. By maintaining a consistent water supply, plants can establish stronger root systems, develop healthier foliage, and produce more abundant blooms or fruits.

Furthermore, the convenience and flexibility of drip irrigation are evident through its easy automation capabilities. By incorporating timers or controllers, the watering process can be automated, providing plants with consistent and optimal moisture levels. This feature proves particularly beneficial for busy individuals or those who may be away from their gardens for extended periods. With automated drip irrigation, plants can thrive and receive adequate water even in the absence of regular monitoring.

By implementing drip irrigation in your garden, you can optimize water usage, support plant health, and create an environment where your plants can flourish.

CHAPTER 8: PRUNING STRATEGIES FOR EXTENDED FLOWERING

Most plants should have their old foliage cut back in early spring, just after the blooms have faded. Many perennials that bloom in spring should be trimmed at this time. Perennials that bloom in summer and autumn should be pruned in spring to encourage bushier growth and more abundant flowering. While deadheading spent flowers benefits most perennials, not all perennials respond well to pruning before they bloom, as it may remove the only blooms of the year. Continue reading to discover how to prune, what to prune, how to strengthen plants, get more flowers, and when to prune them.

- Deadheading Technique

Two of the most important reasons for pruning perennials are extending the bloom duration and encouraging recurrent flowering. By removing fading or spent flowers, known as deadheading, you can prolong or encourage the reblooming of your garden's flowers. When the plant is prevented from setting seeds, it often directs its energy towards producing new flowers to complete its life cycle. Deadheading redirects the plant's energy towards new flower production rather than seed production. Deadheading is beneficial for many perennials, including Stoke's Aster, Phlox, Black-eyed Susan, Columbine, and Phlox. To deadhead a faded flower, pinch off the flower stem below the spent bloom and above the first set of leaves. If there are multiple blooms in a cluster, shear the entire plant back.

- Technique for Perennial Pruning Compact Plants with More Flowers

Utilize this method to decrease plant height and create bushier, more flower-bearing plants that don't need staking. Pinching helps certain perennial plants stay more compact and promotes more blooms. Pruning will also shorten the plant's height, making staking unnecessary. Branching is promoted by pruning. Two stems will grow for each one pruned back, increasing the number of blossoms. Cutting down or pinching perennials before they blossom can save you time later on when you need to stake the plants and will result in more flowers. Flowers on pruned flower stems may bloom 2–3 weeks later than usual and may be smaller. Phlox, Mums, Asters, Sedums, Beebalm, Monkshood, Joe-Pye Weed, and Sneezeweed are a few examples of plants that benefit. Cut down 1/3 to 1/2 of the plant's top growth in the spring. Fall-blooming plants need to be pruned by July 4th.

- Technique for Perennial Pruning to Promote New Growth

Utilize this method to promote luxuriant new growth and re-bloom. Plants should be pruned after blooming and whenever the old growth starts to look ragged to encourage lush new growth from the root system. This fresh growth helps enhance the garden's overall aesthetic, renewing it and maintaining its position in the overall design. Sometimes, a plant may even blossom again after being pruned almost all the way to the ground. Salvia, Spiderwort, Catmint, and Perennial Geranium are a few examples of plants that benefit from this practice. Look for fresh growth emerging from the plant's base beneath the worn-out growth. When pruning, leave the crown or at least 2" of the old stems as you cut the plant back to the new growth.

- Technique for Perennial Pruning for Double Bloom Time

Utilize this method to stagger plant bloom period and height while extending bloom time with more blooms. By pinching or pruning back perennials that are grouped together, you can encourage the plants to reach maturity at various heights or bloom at slightly different intervals. This prolongs the bloom period, adds more blooms, and creates intriguing gradations. Flowering can be delayed to extend the bloom duration on a few stems of a single plant. Pinching causes a 2- to 3-week delay in flowering for many perennials. Examples of plants that can be controlled by pruning include Phlox, Beebalm, Asters, Mums, Sneezeweed, Chelone, Obedient Plant, Veronica, Joe-Pye Weed, Russian Sage, Catmint, and Monkshood.

If the front half of a perennial cluster is pruned, the rear half will bloom first at its usual time. Later blooming will occur in the pruned front section. When the rear half is finished blooming, the blossoming front will conceal it. Alternatively, you can pinch back half of the bloom stems throughout the entire cluster. Pinch

spring bloomers for summer bloomers. Fall-blooming plants should be pruned by July 4th.

- Technique for Perennial Pruning to Increase the Flower Size

A plant will produce a single, large bloom on a long stalk if the side buds are cut off or disbudded. For certain plants, thinning the stems might result in blooms that are bigger than those from unthinned plants.

When Should Perennials Be Pinch?

By cutting down the flower stems of many perennials, you can postpone blossoming by two to three weeks. Perennials can be timed to bloom in waves by carefully trimming them. Perennial plants that bloom in the spring shouldn't be clipped until after blossoming. Early in the spring, pinch back summer bloomers. By July 4th, prune perennials with autumn blooms. These include mums, chelone, and asters. Plants that benefit from pruning include Aconitums, Achillea, Adenophora, Alcea, Aegopodium,

Amsonia, Arabis, Anchusa, Artemisia, Boltonias, Asters, Campanulas, Centranthus, Centaurea, Clematis, Chrysanthemums, Coreopsis, Eupatorium, Helianthus, Gypsophila, Heliopsis, Leucanthemum, Iberis, Linum, Monarda, Lobelias, Perovskia, Physostegia, Phlox paniculata, Platycodon, Saponaria, Salvias, Stokesia, Thalictrum, Tanacetum, Veronicas, and Tradescantia.

Benefits of Pruning for Year-Round Blooming

Improved Airflow: Pruning helps create better airflow within the plant canopy by removing crowded or crossing branches. This improved circulation reduces the risk of fungal diseases, as it allows for increased evaporation of moisture on leaves and minimizes humidity levels. Adequate airflow also helps plants access carbon dioxide, a key component in photosynthesis, leading to healthier growth and increased flower production.

Enhanced Light Penetration: By selectively pruning branches, especially those that are dense or shading other parts of the plant, light can reach lower areas of the plant and encourage balanced growth. Increased light penetration stimulates the production of chlorophyll, promoting robust photosynthesis and providing plants with the energy they need to thrive. With more access to light, plants are more likely to produce an abundance of vibrant blooms.

Better Nutrient Distribution: Pruning helps redirect the flow of nutrients within the plant. By removing excess or competing branches, the plant can allocate resources more efficiently to essential areas such as developing flower buds. This optimal nutrient distribution supports healthy flower development and encourages more prolific blooming.

Structural Integrity: Pruning plays a crucial role in maintaining the structural integrity of plants. Removing weak, damaged, or diseased branches reduces the risk of breakage and prevents potential harm to the plant or surrounding structures. By promoting a well-balanced framework, pruning ensures that plants can withstand external forces such as wind, rain, or heavy flower loads without compromising their overall health.

Size Control: Pruning allows for size management, especially for plants that tend to grow vigorously or exceed the desired

dimensions in a garden space. Regular pruning helps maintain a compact and manageable size, preventing overcrowding and facilitating easier maintenance. By controlling the size of plants, gardeners can create a harmonious and aesthetically pleasing landscape that accommodates other plants and features.

Encourages New Growth: Pruning stimulates the growth of new branches and lateral buds, leading to a fuller and denser plant form. By selectively removing older or spent branches, the plant redirects resources towards new growth, resulting in increased branching and a greater number of potential flower buds. This rejuvenation process rejuvenates the plant, rejuvenating its vigor and encouraging robust flowering.

Pruning is an essential technique in gardening that involves selectively removing parts of plants to enhance their health, shape, and productivity. Understanding the fundamental concepts and principles of pruning is crucial for achieving successful results.

Here's an overview:

Purpose of Different Pruning Cuts:

Thinning: Thinning cuts involve removing entire branches or stems at their point of origin, usually back to a lateral branch or the main stem. Thinning reduces plant density, improves airflow, and allows light to penetrate, resulting in better overall plant health.

Heading: Heading cuts remove a portion of a branch, typically just above a bud or lateral branch. This type of cut stimulates new growth, branching, and flower production.

Rejuvenation: Rejuvenation cuts involve severe pruning, often cutting back the plant to its base or main framework. This technique is used to renew overgrown or neglected plants, promoting vigorous regrowth and revitalizing the plant's overall health.

Timing and Reasons for Pruning Different Plants:

Deciduous Trees and Shrubs: Prune during late winter or early spring before new growth emerges. Pruning goals may include shaping, removing dead or damaged branches, stimulating flowering or fruit production, or controlling size.

Evergreen Trees and Shrubs: Pruning is generally done in early spring, but the timing can vary based on specific species. Goals may include shaping, removing diseased or pest-infested branches, maintaining density, or promoting new growth.

<u>Flowering Plants:</u> Timing depends on the plant's flowering pattern. Prune spring-flowering plants immediately after blooming to avoid removing buds, while prune summer-flowering plants during late winter or early spring. Objectives include removing spent blooms, shaping, controlling size, and promoting vigorous growth.

<u>Fruit Trees:</u> Pruning is typically performed during late winter or early spring. Goals include managing tree shape, improving light penetration, removing diseased or damaged branches, and stimulating fruit production.

<u>Hedges and Topiaries:</u> Prune hedges and topiaries throughout the growing season to maintain shape and density.

Light pruning can be done regularly, while more severe pruning is usually performed during late winter or early spring.

Importance of Proper Tools and Techniques:

<u>Clean and Sharp Tools:</u> Use clean and sharp pruning tools to ensure precise cuts that minimize damage to plants. Dull or dirty tools can cause crushing or tearing of plant tissues, making plants more susceptible to diseases and slower to heal.

Cutting Techniques: Employ proper cutting techniques, such as making clean cuts at the correct angle just above a bud or lateral branch. Avoid leaving stubs or cutting too close to the bud, as it may damage or kill it.

Tool Selection: Choose the right tools for the job based on the plant's size and the type of cut needed. Examples include hand pruners, loppers, pruning saws, and hedge shears. Using the appropriate tool ensures efficient and effective pruning.

By understanding the purpose of different pruning cuts, considering the timing and reasons for pruning specific plants, and using proper tools and techniques, gardeners can promote plant health, control growth, shape plants to desired forms, and encourage optimal flowering or fruiting. Pruning is a skill that, when applied correctly, contributes to the overall beauty, health, and longevity of garden plants.

Pruning Techniques for Different Flower Varieties

Pruning Perennials:

Deadheading: Remove spent flowers by cutting them back to a lateral bud or leaf. This promotes continuous blooming and prevents seed formation, directing the plant's energy towards producing new blooms.

Dividing: Some perennials benefit from dividing every few years to rejuvenate and prevent overcrowding. Dig up the plant, carefully separate the clumps, and replant the divided sections, ensuring each division has healthy roots and shoots.

Pruning Annuals:

Pinching: Pinching involves removing the top portion of young plants, typically with fingers or shears, to encourage branching and compact growth. Pinching can be repeated as the plant grows to maintain a bushier form.

Deadheading: Similar to perennials, remove spent flowers to redirect energy towards continuous blooming. Annuals often produce more blooms when deadheaded regularly.

Pruning Shrubs:

Shearing: Use hedge shears to shape shrubs, creating clean, formal lines or desired shapes. Shearing is commonly done on evergreen shrubs, such as boxwood or privet, to maintain a specific form or size.

Selective Pruning: Thin out crowded branches or remove dead or damaged wood to improve air circulation and overall plant health. Make pruning cuts just above a bud or lateral branch.

Pruning Climbers:

Training: Direct the growth of climbers by tying or training them to a support structure, such as a trellis or arbor. Gently secure the stems using soft ties, allowing the plant to climb and spread evenly.

Thinning: For climbers that become dense or tangled, selectively remove some older or inward-growing branches to improve airflow and promote better flower production.

Step-by-Step Instructions for Pruning Flower Varieties:

Roses: Remove dead, damaged, or crossing branches in late winter or early spring. Make clean cuts just above an outward-facing bud, angled away from the bud.

Hydrangeas: Prune specific types according to their flowering characteristics. Remove dead wood, thin out overcrowded branches, and cut back old wood to encourage new growth and abundant blooms.

Clematis: Pruning requirements vary depending on the clematis group (e.g., Group 1, 2, or 3). Follow specific guidelines for each group, which may include light pruning, cutting back to a set of strong buds, or more severe pruning.

Lilies: After flowering, remove spent flowers, but allow the foliage to die back naturally. Cut back the stems to the ground once they have turned yellow or brown.

Geraniums: Trim back leggy or spent stems to encourage compact growth and continuous blooming. Cut just above a set of healthy leaves or nodes.

Timing and Frequency of Pruning

It is important to note that while this guide provides general recommendations, specific plants may have unique pruning requirements.

Deciduous Trees and Shrubs:

Pruning Timing: Late winter or early spring, before new growth begins.

Frequency: Once a year.

Why: Pruning during dormancy promotes vigorous regrowth in the upcoming growing season, optimizes resource allocation, and reduces stress on the plant.

Evergreen Trees and Shrubs:

Pruning Timing: Timing varies by species but is generally done in early spring.

Frequency: Once a year or as needed.

Why: Pruning in early spring allows sufficient time for recovery and new growth before summer. It also provides better visibility of the plant's structure when the leaves are absent.

Spring-Flowering Plants:

Pruning Timing: Prune immediately after flowering.

Frequency: Once a year.

Why: Pruning after flowering allows the plant to set new buds for the next season. Delayed pruning may remove buds and hinder next year's bloom.

Summer-Flowering Plants:

Pruning Timing: Late winter or early spring.

Frequency: Once a year.

Why: Pruning before new growth helps direct energy toward new shoots, leading to robust growth and abundant blooms in the upcoming summer.

Fruit Trees:

Pruning Timing: Late winter or early spring, before bud break.

Frequency: Annually or as needed.

Why: Pruning during dormancy stimulates new growth, improves fruit production, enhances overall tree health, and aids in shaping the tree's structure and canopy.

Hedges and Topiaries:

Pruning Timing: Throughout the growing season.

Frequency: Regularly, based on desired shape and growth rate.

Why: Regular pruning maintains the desired form, encourages dense growth, and light, frequent pruning is preferable to infrequent, severe pruning for hedges and topiaries.

In addition to the general guidelines, it is important to observe specific plant cues:

Bud Formation: Prune after flowers have faded to avoid removing developing buds.

Dormancy: Prune deciduous plants when they are dormant, before the new growth emerges.

Regrowth: Prune when new growth begins to ensure the plant allocates resources appropriately.

Overall, pruning is a valuable gardening technique that promotes healthy growth, enhances the appearance of plants, and increases flower production. By understanding the pruning needs of different plant varieties, employing appropriate techniques, and adhering to the proper timing, gardeners can maximize the beauty and productivity of their flower gardens."

Pruning Dos and Don'ts:

Dos:

- Do understand the plant: Take the time to familiarize yourself with the specific pruning requirements and growth habits of each plant species in your garden. Different plants may have different pruning needs.

- Do use clean and sharp tools: Ensure that your pruning tools are clean, sterilized, and sharp. This helps to make precise cuts and prevents the introduction of pathogens or damage to the plant.

- Do make clean cuts: When pruning, make smooth and clean cuts just above a bud or lateral branch. Avoid leaving stubs or ragged edges, as they can attract pests and diseases.

- Do prune for a purpose: Before you start pruning, have a clear objective in mind. Whether it's to remove dead or damaged wood, improve airflow, or shape the plant, pruning with a specific goal will help you achieve the desired results.

- Do observe plant cues: Pay attention to the plant's cues such as bud formation, dormancy periods, and specific flowering patterns. Prune at the appropriate time to avoid interfering with future blooms or stressing the plant.

- Do step back and evaluate: Regularly step back and assess the overall shape and structure of the plant. Prune with an eye for maintaining a balanced and healthy form.

Don'ts:

- Don't over-prune: Avoid excessive pruning as it can weaken the plant and reduce its ability to produce energy through photosynthesis. Prune conservatively, removing only what is necessary.

- Don't prune too late or too early: Pruning at the wrong time can disrupt flowering or growth cycles. Research and understand the appropriate pruning times for each specific plant.

- Don't neglect tool maintenance: Keep your pruning tools clean, sharp, and well-maintained. Regularly oil moving parts, sharpen blades, and replace worn-out or damaged tools to ensure clean cuts.

- Don't neglect safety: Always prioritize safety when pruning. Wear appropriate protective gear, such as gloves and safety glasses, to prevent injuries. Be cautious when using sharp tools and when working at heights.

- Don't ignore overall plant care: Pruning is just one aspect of plant care. Remember to address other essential needs, such as watering, fertilizing, and pest control, to maintain overall plant health.

- Don't prune in extreme weather conditions: Avoid pruning during extreme heat, cold, or wet weather. Extreme conditions can stress the plant and hinder its ability to recover from pruning cuts.

Maintaining Balance:

Find a balance between pruning and overall plant care. While pruning is important, it should be integrated into a comprehensive approach that includes proper watering, fertilization, and soil health to support long-term plant vitality.

Regularly monitor and assess the health and growth of your plants. Adjust pruning practices as needed based on the plant's response and specific requirements.

By following these dos and avoiding common pruning mistakes, you can promote plant health, achieve desired shapes, and support the long-term vitality and beauty of your garden. Remember, each plant is unique, so understanding their needs and providing appropriate care is key to successful pruning.

CHAPTER 9: HOW TO PROTECT YOUR GARDEN FROM PEST & DISEASES?

There are several strategies to safeguard your garden and lower the chance of damage from pests and diseases. Natural methods are the most effective ways to stop invasive insect infestations and plant diseases. Your plants will develop healthier if you give them basic upkeep and attention. Infected and diseased plants are less likely to be healthy. You can start adopting some healthy habits right now to maintain the health of your garden or landscape.

Maintain a clutter-free and tidy landscape.

In order to be ready for spring, when all the creepy crawlies awaken from their long winter hibernation, it is extremely crucial to do this chore in the winter. Potent insect eggs may be present in your yard's dead plant matter and leaves. Fungal spores may also reside in garden waste. Eliminating pests, diseases, and yard debris without using pesticides or other treatments is essential. One of the best ways to address the question, 'How can

I protect my plants from insects naturally?' is by properly maintaining the area where your plants are grown. After weeding, trimming, or raking, twigs, piles of leaves, or other waste can become a haven for new life. A pile of dried leaves or twigs creates the perfect warm, dark habitat for bacteria, fungi, and insect larvae. The decomposition of organic materials provides an ideal environment for the emergence of new fungi, bacteria, and insects. However, certain bacteria, fungi, and insects benefit the health of the garden. You can start composting or mulching using the decaying vegetable waste from your garden. Keep your compost a fair distance away from the plants since invasive pests and plant diseases can thrive in decaying organic debris.

- Water plants' bases to prevent fungus problems.

Many plants are more susceptible to fungal infestation when watered from above. If you must water plants from above, water them in the early hours rather than at night so that the water can evaporate off the leaves. Good watering practices are among the best methods to help plants fight diseases. An excess of water can promote fungal growth. However, insufficient water can make it difficult for your plants to stay healthy, leading to various other issues. Lack of water can cause plants to withhold nutrients from parts of their leaves, blooms, or fruit. As a result, the plant's components may start to rot and die, attracting insect infestations. It is recommended to water tropical plants that require moisture from above, such as citrus plants.

- Keep the plants in good shape.

Weak plants are more susceptible to attacks by pests and diseases. When you ask, 'How can I naturally protect my plants from insects?' keeping plants healthy is one of the best methods to prevent illness or pest infestations. Recognize and implement the specific needs of your plants regarding water, spacing, trimming, and fertilization.

Ensuring suitable soil conditions for your plants is the first step. By regularly checking the levels of acids and alkalis, you can maintain the health of your soil. Crop rotation techniques are also excellent measures to prevent nutrient depletion and promote replenishment. This may seem unusual for a flower garden since flowers are not precisely crops. However, certain flower and garden-friendly plant varieties deplete specific soil nutrients, while others replenish them. Crop rotation has been used to maintain plant health since the sickle, the second-oldest agricultural tool ever found through archaeology, after the plough.

Plants have several natural defense mechanisms built-in, some of which are more potent than anything humans can do to help them. Keeping the plants healthy enhances the effectiveness of these built-in defense mechanisms. If plants are not struggling with excessive sunlight, insufficient water, or poor soil, they are more likely to fend off illnesses or fungal invasions. Take care of your plants! Ensure they receive the nutrients, water, and sunlight they require.

- Plant things that keep pests away or even repel them.

Unwanted insects that destroy your plants are repelled by plants like petunias, rosemary, chrysanthemums, garlic, and chives. Plant irises if you want to stop deer from devouring your flowers. Deer avoid them at all costs.

Although it is natural to expect flowers to attract insects, certain plants produce smells that deter them.

While pepper spray may be useful in fending off some dangerous insects, the majority of natural pesticides only act when insects are present. Spray made from hot peppers may be used as an efficient prophylactic method to ward off insects. Many insects dislike pepper because of its chemistry, giving it the flavor humans often find appealing. Hot pepper spray is safe for many plants in small doses, however. Pepper spray is a good preventative method against bug infestations. If you're thinking, "How do I keep flies away from my plants?" you could find the remedy you seek in pepper spray.

- Using mulch is a terrific approach to saving water and safeguarding the roots of your plants.

With the aid of mulch, your plants can get the moisture they need without the ground becoming excessively wet. Mulch should never touch the branches of the trees, shrubs, or trunk when applied. Mulch should not be piled up against the foundation of the house. Mulching benefits the overall health of the plants. It also helps prevent fungus-related diseases that thrive in overly humid conditions. Additionally, mulch provides a habitat for beneficial insects, allowing them to control invasive insects.

- Select plants that are resistant to pests and/or diseases, particularly if you are aware of a problem in your neighbourhood.

Look for plants that can withstand that specific problem. This is crucial when it comes to harmful fungal illnesses. Do some research on the plants you want to grow. Some strains or types of plants will be more resilient to fungal invasions or plant diseases. When choosing what to grow, consider your environment.

- To stop any recurring illnesses, use chemicals like fungicides or neem oil.

It might be tough to get rid of fungal infections. The best course of action for this type of disease is prevention. To control insects, use pesticides, and to treat mites, use miticides. Consider using natural pesticides like Neem oil, pyrethrins, soapy water, etc., while learning how to protect plants from insects organically. The market is flooded with solutions for invasive insect infestations and plant diseases. When purchasing these products, you should exercise caution and choose something safe for the plants.

How to Maintain Healthy Soil and Nutrient Balance

The function of soil composition in terms of supporting plant development and health is referred to as soil health. The three primary characteristics of soil—biological, physical, and nutritive—that may be influenced and altered are the subjects of this useful advice and gardening techniques. Gardeners may attempt to produce better soil in their backyard gardens.

Know how your soil looks and feels.

It is time well spent to feel the soil in your garden with your hands and carefully analyze it since 50% of the soil comprises its physical structure. Using these field observations, you can identify the soil's structure, texture, and workability. Rub a tiny bit of dirt between your fingers to feel the texture. When moist, sandy soil crumbles and feels rough and abrasive. Silt is smooth and slippery while wet but feels silky or floury when dry. When damp, clay has a slippery, gooey feeling before drying into firm clods that often have fissures in the topsoil. Examine a big clump of dirt that has been dug up. Healthy soil has a crumbly or granular texture. It will form clumps, and loose soil fragments, plant roots, and decomposing organic materials may adhere to them. When the soil is overly damp, it becomes weakened when worked. Press a small amount of soil firmly in your hands. Workable soil easily crumbles. When the soil is overly damp, it becomes compacted, sticky, or muddy, and it is not suitable for planting and digging. Working the soil in this condition will cause it to crust and harden, further damaging its structure if it is predominantly clay or silt. Therefore, overly damp soil should not be worked since it will be ruined.

Feed Organic Matter to Your Soil

An adequate amount of organic matter is one of the most crucial indicators of healthy soil. Adding organic matter to your soil enriches the garden soil. Add organic materials when creating a new garden bed, expanding an existing one, or planting fresh flowers. In the top six to twelve inches of your garden bed, or even deeper in a landscaping bed, rototill or dig in between one and three inches of organic matter. Working with organic materials is best done in the autumn, as they will have time to decay throughout the winter.

Typical organic soil additions include the following:

- Home composting organic matter

- Compost made from the substrate (such as mushroom soil) that mushrooms have used up.

- Peat moss

- Aged/dried animal manure

- Shredded leaves

- Humus

The features of organic materials vary. For instance, peat moss lacks inherent nutrients, but old composts and dry manures do contain them. Although peat moss has a higher acidic pH than compost, there is no evidence to suggest that it reduces the soil pH. Typically, mushroom dung has an alkaline pH. Some may think that wood chips, animal manures, and sawdust are too fresh. However, since nitrogen is significantly utilized during the breakdown process, using them as a soil amendment can tie up soil nitrogen. It is advised to compost extremely coarse tree bark, wood chips, and sawdust for 1 or 2 years before incorporating them into the soil. When purchasing organic material, always check the actual contents to know what is in the bag. When buying compost in bulk, make sure it was produced according to the recommended temperature and duration for composting.

Good garden soils that contain an adequate amount of organic matter exhibit certain characteristics: a good open structure with a granular appearance, less compacted soil, and increased permeability for plant roots. Sandy soils may retain more water and nutrients because the organic content prevents microscopic particles like clay from forming a solid mass, whether wet or dry. The proportion of organic matter can be determined through a Penn State soil test upon request. If the soil test's relative cation exchange capacity (CEC) indicates less than 15, it is recommended to add at least 1 inch of organic matter to the soil.

Protect the Soil with Organic Mulching

Mulches are applied to plant soil in a uniform layer. Mulching is a highly beneficial gardening practice when done correctly.

Organic mulches protect and strengthen garden soil by doing the following:

- Preserving soil moisture by shielding the soil from the sun.

- Limiting excessive seasonal temperature fluctuations.

- Decomposing, thus supplying nutrients (organic matter!) and enhancing structure.

- Reducing weed germination and development.

- Preserving moderate runoff and rain.

For use in the backyard garden, many types of organic mulch materials are available, such as hardwood or shredded bark, shredded leaves, 12-inch pine needles, screened compost, coarse wood chips, pine bark nuggets, and straw. The performance benefits come from a sufficient and consistent layer of bark/hardwood or screened compost ingredients.

Mulching garden beds is best done in the middle of spring. Eliminate weeds, tidy up plant waste (and add it to your compost pile). Spread an even layer of organic materials about 2 to 4 inches thick over the garden soil. To avoid laying down too much mulch, consider any leftovers from the previous season. Keep all mulch three to five inches away from the base of a shrub or tree's stems or trunk when mulching around it. Mulch contacting the branches and trunks of shrubs may harm the plants, causing them to deteriorate or even die.

Synthetic (non-organic) mulches, including ornamental stone, gravel, and landscaping textiles, are available. Synthetic mulches are durable, but unlike organic mulches, they do not improve the condition of the soil. Gravel and stones absorb heat, drying up the soil and potentially harming the soil's beneficial microbes. Weeds can start growing when airborne weed seeds fall between the gravel and stones. Landscape textiles protect the garden soil but can be troublesome as they may restrict water and biological activity in the soil and deteriorate over time.

- Take care while walking on the ground and tilling the soil.

Too much foot traffic, the use of large machinery, and other heavy loads may compress the soil, particularly when the soil is moist or saturated. So, be sure to handle the soil in your garden with care. Stay on the paths, keep garden carts there, and avoid parking or using heavy vehicles on the grass. Don't dig, plant, or walk on the garden soil in the spring until it is dry. Compaction can also result from excessive mechanical rototilling because it negatively affects the soil aggregates. The soil may initially seem loose and crumbly after rototilling, but if it is watered and walked on during planting, the soil can easily compact and become firm. Compaction reduces the pore space and disrupts the soil's aggregate structure. This can lead to poor water infiltration, erosion, runoff, and puddling in your garden. In compacted soil, plant roots may struggle to grow and access oxygen, water, and nutrients.

- Perform a soil test to be fertile!

Understanding a soil's nutrients is equivalent to understanding its fertility.

For optimum plant development, the available nutrients must be balanced. A soil fertility test, accessible through your local Penn State Extension office, is the only way to be certain.

The macronutrients phosphate (P), calcium (Ca), potassium (K), and magnesium (Mg) are measured in the soil. Depending on the planned crop, it also provides a nitrogen (N) recommendation. Additionally, the relative cation exchange capacity (CEC) of the soil and soil pH, which influence the soil's release of nutrients and measure the soil's ability to store nutrients, are reported.

Upon request, the proportion of organic matter is provided. Correction advice is also given for any abnormal findings. Recommendations often include a fertilizer comprising nutrients like nitrogen (N), phosphorus (P), and potassium (K), along with the requirement for lime, magnesium, and other nutrients.

- Minimise or Avoid Pesticide Use

Are you aware that a well-kept garden seldom ever requires pesticides? Insects are common on outdoor garden plants, but most of them cause little or no harm.

Additionally, most pests have corresponding beneficial bugs that want to eat them. Normally, healthy soil contains a thriving population of helpful microbes. Take care of your garden and observe closely. If you notice a pest issue, use a systematic approach to determine if a pesticide is necessary.

CHAPTER 10: STEP-BY-STEP GUIDE AND INSPIRATIONS

Flowers make us feel happy and comforted. They also help us enter a meditative state of mind when we smell them. What do they ask for in return? Nothing! Even if their petals are fading to brown, they still give, even if you choose to let them wither away. You can employ a few techniques to prolong the blooming of your plants. This book will provide detailed instructions and inspiration for your year-round garden.

Step-by-step Guide to Year-round Success

A year-round gardening strategy will enable you to extend the harvest to every month of the year. Do you have what it takes to advance your garden? Many gardeners are anxious about year-round gardening because it seems like much additional labor. Why not take the winter off to relax, recover, and have time for other things?

Spring: Awakening the Garden with Early Blommers

This is the ideal moment to plant bulbs as outdoor life thrives. The month of February is very uplifting. The days are getting longer and the garden is clearly waking up. A recurring concern is small bulbs. The first important question is: what happens to them during the summer? Should I disturb the bulbs by digging them up when they should be left in peace to establish where they are? Will they create a visual obstruction? Daffodils with their large leaves become unsightly and cumbersome until June. However, smaller varieties like N. bulbocodium, Narcissus cyclamineus, or our local Lent lily, N. pseudonarcissus, are not a problem. Their leaves are thin and small enough to wither away quickly.

What about the perennials I don't want to disturb for many years, such as eryngiums and Japanese anemones? They benefit from over- or interplanting. You can plant lightweight narcissi, like those classified as triandrus hybrids, among your clumps of daylilies (hemerocallis). As the perennials mature, their strap-like leaves will completely conceal the bulbs.

Deciduous shrubs leave the ground bare and well-lit until their own foliage emerges. For example, you can remove some of the lower branches of Weigela Florida 'Florida Variegata' to give the bulbs more space. This creates room for primroses, sturdy Cyclamen neapolitanum, sweet-scented Viola odorata, whose marbled leaves create beautiful patterns from fall through spring, and violets. Although this assortment may not have an impressive lineage, it is resilient, eager, and multiplies well. The first flowers should be blooming by now, but it's still early.

Colonizing under gnarled trees is challenging. In general, it's not worth cultivating plants that can withstand the dry shade in the summer. They would be better off elsewhere. However, early bulbs that emerge and develop while there is still light and moisture are excellent, especially if you cover them with organic mulch in the fall, such as leaf mold, well-rotted bark, or mushroom compost (provided its alkaline nature won't disrupt anything).

Crocus tommasinianus is an excellent colonizer as it self-seeds wonderfully. Its mauve and slender blooms open up to the sun during this month. Winter aconites, Eranthis hyemalis, may be a challenge for some gardeners. However, many find them to be effortlessly simple, and they make great companions for crocuses beneath a tree, even a beech tree. They also pair well with hostas.

These self-seeding plants are particularly satisfying as they can grow where you wouldn't normally plant them, such as directly in the crown of a still-growing hosta, like H. sieboldiana var. elegans. If you don't mind them mixing with other plants, early bulbs with small leaves look fantastic with roses. A self-seeding, blue-and-white Chionodoxa luciliae, resembling a scilla, filled a bed of hybrid tea roses in a friend's garden. They jokingly referred to it as a weed, but it kept coming back; you shouldn't have any issue with that kind of "weed" at all. Dutch crocuses reach their peak bloom the following month, nestled beneath and among roses. Later on, it's true that their foliage can become messy, but by that time, the roses themselves are not particularly attractive. The crocuses will have faded away by the time the roses take center stage.

Summer: Harnessing the Vibrancy of the Peak Season

One of the four seasons on Earth is summer, which comes after spring and signals the arrival of fall. The days are warm, hot, and exceptionally long during this time of year, while the nights are the shortest. The sun is shining so brightly, and the whole world is beckoning you outside! In summer, everything is blooming, birds are tweeting, and you can feel the surroundings coming alive around you. Nature is drenched in vibrant hues. Fruit-bearing plants and trees, many colorful flowers in bloom, and a wonderful aroma permeating the air are all signs of summer. Animals may breed on warm days with ideal weather! In summer, sunlight is also crucial for plants and trees because it creates optimal conditions for photosynthesis. Plants receive beneficial nourishment during this process, and we subsequently breathe clean air.

The most well-known summer flower is the Begonia, loved by everyone for its large, vibrant flowers and its ability to thrive in both sun and shade throughout the whole summer. Lobelia is an annual summer flower that looks great in gardens and can be used to create stunning cascades of smaller petals. Blue and violet are ever-thriving colors! The optimal time to grow various crops such as beans, maize, celery, cucumbers, broccoli, edamame, muskmelons, okra, and eggplants is also during summer.

Perennial flowers that bloom all summer long are more prevalent than you may think, even though many gardeners consider annuals as their go-to option for a season full of blooms.

Many perennials, such as black-eyed Susans, charming Shasta daisies, dramatic purple and blue asters, and magnificent yellow-gold Stella D'Oro daisies, will start flowering in mid to late summer and continue into autumn. They make excellent cut flowers and bouquet fillers. For lush, mid-height fillers between ground covers and taller plants, hardy "Crane's Bill" geraniums in hues of maroon to purple, bright yellow Sundrop primroses, and spiky blue delphiniums can also bloom for weeks at a time.

A flower-dense ground cover called creeping phlox blooms for weeks on end and spreads (hence the name) a pleasing carpet of white, purple, pink, or blue flowers over rocks, walls, and other garden elements.

Whether used alone or in conjunction with perennials, annual flowers are a simple way to grow a colorful flower garden because they tend to bloom nonstop. The wonderfully flowering samarasin plant continues to bloom throughout the early part of autumn. Fast-growing zinnias with vivid, full blossoms are available in bright orange. Rich burgundy globe amaranth has stalks topped with papery globes that resemble clover and are perfect for drying and cutting. Petunias are low-maintenance plants that bloom from May to September and come in a rainbow of colors and sizes.

They can be used as a mounded ground cover or an overflowing container accent. Impatiens from New Guinea bloom early and don't mind whether they receive full sun, partial shade, or neither. Cheerful, dependable marigolds accentuate garden borders. Moss roses cover the ground and can withstand drought while offering a variety of colors. Their double blossoms have a charming polka-dot pattern. You can plant any annual summer flower in spring or early summer for months of dazzling color. However, remember that young perennials won't bloom in their first year. If you're starting your first summer flower garden and have decided to use perennials, plant some annuals to ensure you have blooms this season.

Autumn: Embracing the Beauty of Fall Blooms

Many more flowers can survive the autumn weather, even if the lowering temperatures often cause the demise of other blooms.

Here is a helpful reference to some flowers that bloom in the autumn: garden fog in the autumn.

A garden is always transformed into a lovely setting when fog takes us to another planet. The delicate hues harmoniously blend, and plants that would have gone unnoticed at other times of the year have their chance to shine.

The Fall Aster lives true to its name by bringing vibrant purple flowers to gardens. The Mexican Mint Marigold serves as both a pleasant herb and a charming flower, with its little yellow blooms adorning any garden or landscape, and its leaves lending a subdued licorice flavor to any cuisine.

The Copper Canyon Daisy is a plant with gorgeous golden blooms that can endure dry conditions. It has a piney scent. Autumn Sage or Salvia Greggii, which can be grown along fences or the sides of buildings without any problems, will draw hummingbirds to your landscape. Fire Spike, deeply shade-tolerant, has lovely dark green foliage and vivid red tubular blooms that are at their best in the autumn. Mexican Bush Sage can withstand low moisture levels and wow gardeners with its pale purple blossoms. Dianthus, Petunias, snapdragons, and calendula are among the annuals that flourish in our warm autumn weather and last far into the winter or even beyond.

These autumn blossoms will give a colorful boost to the landscaping at your house. In addition to your usual gardening practices, bear in mind that certain places may still have stringent watering restrictions in effect due to the decreasing weather. Keep the watering of your garden within limits. Provide sun-loving plants with the right amount of light while keeping shade-loving plants in the shade.

Winter: Transforming Your Garden into a Winter Wonderland

Before transforming your uninteresting yard into a winter wonderland for a holiday party, you must decide on the theme. It's simple to get confused since many different methods exist to create a wonderland. Setting a theme will thus enable you to concentrate on creating unified designs. Your visitors will be astounded by the idea of Santa's village or fascinating nativity displays. Before choosing a theme, you should also take into account the available area in your garden. Simple winter decorations may work well if it's a tiny space. However, if you have a large lawn, you might consider some unique ideas for decorating it.

Cleaning your yard is the next step.

The importance of making sanitary preparations cannot be overstated when you are planning a Christmas party in a winter wonderland.

There is seldom a better opportunity to give your garden a complete cleaning. Trim your lawn nicely to add structure, eliminate all the wild grass, and sweep the ground to remove the waste and leaves from autumn.

Although you may assume winter flowers don't exist, the opposite is actually true. Even in cold weather, vegetation can flourish. But if you want to double your yard's attractiveness with winter flowers, you must lay their foundation down many weeks before the party's date. Your visitors will pause to admire your creative outdoor décor because of the lovely flower and snow combination. To add even more excitement to your Winterland, we've also included some winter flora you can cultivate.

1. Chaenomeles: Often known as blooming quinces, blossom throughout late winter and early spring. They are an excellent option for enhancing your winter landscape since they can withstand extreme temperatures. This bloom can reach a height of at

least three meters in China. It also has lovely bouquets of pink and white flowers. The white flowers serve the winter wonderland motif well. Adding a complementary pink tint is a modest yet intriguing way to upgrade your décor.

2. Boxwood: While white hues should be your main emphasis when decorating for winter, a bit of green won't hurt. Consider planting boxwood in your garden. It can reach heights of up to 15 feet on average. The combination of yellow and dark green foliage will add to the festive atmosphere. Depending on the available space in your yard, you can plant boxwood as a small tree or a widely distributed shrub.

3. Winterberry: People passing by will enjoy the appearance of the plant's adorable small red berries. Additionally, you can give your visitors some delicious berries from the shrub. Before you grow this shrub in your garden, it's important to take into account a few factors. It should be planted in a location with partial or full sun protection. For the

winterberry plants to grow quickly, they need at least 6 to 8 hours of sunshine daily.

4. Witch hazel: It flowers throughout late autumn and early winter. You may plant this small tree in your yard before putting up your holiday decorations. The adorable small flowers with pale yellow threads are the perfect way to liven up your drab winter yard.

You can also add fake snow. In the event that it isn't snowing naturally where you are, you may need to arrange for artificial snow. You can purchase fake snow online to help with that. However, such snow won't last long if you reside in a warm climate. Therefore, you should consider this factor before spending money on artificial snow. Renting a snowmaker can be the solution if you want to have real snow.

CHAPTER 11: CREATING YOUR PERSONALIZED YEAR-ROUND BLOOMING HAVEN

Follow these easy instructions to build a garden full of beautiful plants year-round.

- Think About Foliage Before Flowers

Typically, a plant's foliage lasts much longer than its flowers. As landscape designer Karen Chapman suggests in her jointly written book, "Gardening with Foliage First," create a plot with foliage as the main focus. She claims, "If the foliage is lovely, you'll immediately feel joyful." After that, add layers of flowers, berries, and bark to enhance the structure. It is also advised to be open to various cultivars with different leaf characteristics. For instance, if you appreciate how weigela's spring blossoms attract hummingbirds, consider looking for a variegated form or one with dark-colored foliage.

- Build Up the Structure
  Wintertime annual beds seem desolate. Add a border of low-growing junipers or a background of broadleaf evergreens

to make your summer blooms stand out. These shrubs will have sufficient presence in more sedate winter gardens to stand independently.

- Color Waves in Layers

You are not required to use plants that are beautiful all year round if you have a four-season garden. That won't only restrict your options; it may also make your garden seem stagnant and monotonous. Try succession planting instead. This method keeps your preferred fleeting flowers while attractively blending plants from one season to the next. Growing new plants over any remaining leaves from the spring bulbs is one method to employ succession planting. Plant a few late-emerging perennials, such as daylilies, over the bulbs. Be careful not to disturb them by digging too deeply. Next, notice any substantial patches of perennials or annuals. Put spring bulbs between the plants in the autumn. For spring blossoms, plant these tulip bulbs in the autumn. Or, if there is room, you may add some bushes for structure. The walking stick by Harry Lauder is a fantastic option for year-round interest.

- Pick a Palette

Choosing a color and using it consistently throughout the seasons is the simplest approach to creating a unified design. Include a plant with fall-turning orange leaves nearby, such as small bluestem grass (Schizachyrium scoparium). Last but not least, the possumhaw holly (Ilex decidua) sparkles in winter with its vivid orange-red berries. Additionally, birds are drawn to the holly, grass, and hyssop. Think about including these perennials in your garden for year-round bird benefits.

- Include portable motivation

Containers are a quick fix for barren areas at the moment. You can use pots filled with tropical plants with striking leaves to create structure in your garden. A landscape focused on texture will last longer. It is suggested to replace the pots throughout the year with blooming plants and seasonal colors. Purchase portable, compact plants to add brightness to areas that appear barren or dull during certain seasons.

- Prepare a View

You may take pleasure in admiring the snow-draped branches of trees in your yard during winter from afar. However, it is practical to consider planting species with captivating winter features in areas that are easily visible from your windows. This way, you can enjoy their beauty without having to brave the cold and venture far into the garden on chilly days. For the summer, surround outdoor sitting spaces with lush landscaping.

You have the opportunity to experience the unique delights of each month by cultivating a four-season garden. With a little advance preparation, you can create a year-round sanctuary to enjoy with the birds and other animals that live there.

How to Overcome Challenges and Celebrate Your Success

I want you to keep in mind that gardening is a journey rather than a goal when it seems scarier than enjoyable. In a year, you won't be able to learn all there is to know. Even though I have knowledge about gardening, I still don't know everything, and I never will. However, I know more now than yesterday and will know more tomorrow. That motivates me to get out of bed in the morning and keeps me enthusiastic. There will be difficulties in gardening, but each difficulty is a chance to learn a little more. You'll develop into a better, wiser, and more confident gardener as you go. Listed below are some gardening challenges that you may face:

- I'm unsure about what to plant and when.

Several gardeners felt restricted because they were unsure of what to plant and when to plant it. Understanding the seasons is necessary for overcoming this obstacle, which requires practice, knowledge, and the willingness to make errors (I like to see errors as "learning opportunities" since doing so is how we become better gardeners).

Although plants are considerably more robust than we usually give them credit for, they have favored growth seasons, and their ability to withstand extremes of heat and cold is limited. Your frost-free date should be the first thing you search for if you are having trouble comprehending the precise timeframe where you reside. After that point in spring, there is no longer a chance of frost until autumn. In many situations, the plants that will thrive outside are determined by that day. Your region's first autumn frost date is also crucial. Calculate the time a plant will have to develop before the first frosts and work backward from there. Although having this information is crucial, don't allow it to stop you from pushing the envelope. Your garden's microclimate—the particular environment where you live—could be advantageous to you. The risk is minimal for the price of a bag of seeds or a few seedlings, so try it and see what happens.

- The supplies I didn't purchase

Although creating a garden from scratch may seem expensive, it can be done on a tight budget. Don't allow the resources you lack to prevent you from moving forward. You'll discover that you can get by with less, and many resources are free. You can establish a fresh garden for your family with just a $25 budget to demonstrate that it is possible. You can use pizza boxes as makeshift seed trays and make your own seed-starting materials.

You can also obtain free municipal compost made from the leaves the city has collected for soil preparation. Additionally, you can utilize timber from the deconstruction of an old barn. You won't believe how many opportunities there are to acquire free materials and equipment if you set your mind to it. Many people who started gardening but stopped may be glad to offer you their unwanted items rather than having them end up in a landfill.

- There isn't enough room for me to expand.

It suffices to have a garden, regardless of how little land you have to work with. Even the grassy area between the roadway and the sidewalk, known as the "hell strip," is a potential location for a garden. Some of the nicest small gardens I've ever seen have been planted in that little strip, which is only, if you're fortunate, about 18 inches wide. These days, there is an increasing number of plants available that were developed expressly with urban gardeners and their compact areas in mind. Breeders have developed varieties of beloved plants that stop growing when they reach a specific size. Utilizing grow bags is an additional choice. You can grow almost anything in a bag, but the plants won't grow very large since there isn't much room for their roots. You can find solutions that work with your space by searching for "patio plants" and "dwarf plants.

- I put off planning and planting for too long.

Timing is crucial, and as I already indicated, I strongly recommend knowing your frost-free date and first-frost date. The gardening season begins regardless of our level of readiness; it does not wait. It's up to us to be aware of those crucial dates and make the necessary preparations. Your effort to prepare the soil and set up your garden will greatly contribute to its success. But don't underestimate a plant's capacity to catch up. Sometimes you may plant something even if it appears too late, and it will grow to the right size in the summer.

- I'm overwhelmed in the weeds.

As true as death and taxes, weeds are a reality of life. Taming weeds to start a new bed or being forced to weed all summer can be quite demoralizing for many gardeners who detest weeding. I refer to this as "weed overwhelm," and it can be tough to get through. You may find weeding to be extremely Zen, and you might enjoy doing it in the early morning when the garden is at its most serene, or perhaps after a shower when the weeds are easier to spot. You may appreciate the quiet time while gardening rather than listening to podcasts.

The key to weeding is to put on blinkers and concentrate solely on weeding—nothing else will do. You can wander around your garden and pluck weeds for an hour while the timer is set. By breaking the task into manageable portions, it can be prevented from becoming overwhelming. You can focus your weeding efforts in one area before moving on once you're finished. This leaves you with a sense of accomplishment and confidence that you can repeat the same process the next day and make progress.

- I lack sunshine.

Veggies need six to eight hours of direct sunshine daily to develop fruit. Less sunlight in your area might restrict you, but it shouldn't prevent you from planting. Certain plants, including spinach, lettuce, and rocket, can grow food in areas with little sunshine. Focus on shade-loving and -tolerant ornamentals in the meantime, such as ferns, hostas, azaleas, and rhododendrons, etc. Putting the appropriate plant in the right location is an ancient adage in gardening.

- Gardening's primary pain point is pests.

For all gardeners, pests are a concern. You can use various organic pest management techniques, but one of the most effective methods is placing the right plant in the appropriate location. A plant can withstand significant insect damage if it is planted in the right conditions and chosen for your region. An appropriately placed plant will thrive in its surroundings, and a healthy plant will be less prone to pests and diseases. The second most crucial step is taking initiative: Get outside once or twice every day to check on your garden and note any changes. Regular inspections allow you to observe pest activity and take action before it escalates into an infestation. The fewer issues the garden has, the more the gardener's presence is felt in the garden.

Consider the squash vine borer as an example. By taking precautionary steps, such as using a row cover, you can prevent the squash vine borer moth from depositing its eggs on your plants if you are aware of when it enters your garden.

When you have done so much for your garden, it's time to celebrate your achievement.

- Conduct tests, not failures.

Not every attempt you make will be successful. Give yourself permission to try and fail, and make thorough notes so you won't have to strain your memory to recall every detail of the previous season. If you're expanding for business, set aside some areas for testing to prevent unpleasant shocks.

- Commend yourself on the lessons you've learned.

  Focus on what you've learned rather than blaming yourself

over failed blooms or doggedly trying to cultivate a variety in an unsuitable environment. Well done for being a person who can learn from errors! But make notes so you don't keep doing things year after year that don't work. If your tomatoes were planted with the most sunlight and the least amount of shade during the day, the 100-degree summers would blister their leaves. However, a few years ago, they thrived considerably better in the yard's slightly shadier area. To provide them with some shade, you can grow them in pots that you can place closer to your home next year. Maybe, but not really, they like the sun!

- Learn to love your garden planning

The love/hate relationship with making your bedding is complicated. However, the growing season performs better in the years when you give the planning more attention. Giving yourself enough time to plan will enable you to get things started early enough, make necessary adjustments if any "experiments" don't pan out, and enjoy some cozy time daydreaming about how great your garden will be in the middle of winter. Alternatively, choose fall-season vegetables while picturing what it must be like to be cold.

- Identify methods to get outside the house, be present, and appreciate the space you have.

The biggest bed you have, your limited space should be reserved for testing new things. It could be right in the center of your property, making it difficult to conceal from anybody who frequents there. Here you can see where the okra will grow, the beetroot rows you just sown, and how your strawberries will appear after being ravaged by slugs. You may flaunt it even if it isn't "worth" flaunting because I believe there is great value in sharing the unremarkable aspects of life with others.

Spending time slowly in the garden, either while watering or aimlessly weeding, or just relaxing in a nearby chair while reading, I also find to be quite beneficial. It creates room for me to appreciate everything, not only when things are blooming or bearing fruit but also in between.

Gardening serves as a constant reminder to me that it is more important to be present than it is to prepare, take notes, or make a list. I hope you can soon permit yourself to do the same in whatever space you have.

Creating Captivating Color Combinations

Exploring the Artistry of Color Theory in Flower Design

Understanding the principles of color and its profound impact on visual appeal, emotional responses, and sensory experiences is essential in the art of flower design. By delving into the world of color theory, we can masterfully craft arrangements that captivate the senses and convey powerful messages. Let us now explore the fundamentals of color theory and its application in the context of flower design.

The Fundamentals of Color Theory:

Hue: Colors are derived from a wide spectrum of hues found on the color wheel. Ranging from warm tones like red and orange to cool tones like blue and green, hues form the building blocks of color theory.

Saturation: Saturation refers to the intensity or purity of a color. It encompasses vibrant, vivid shades as well as muted, subtle tones.

Value: Value denotes the lightness or darkness of a color. It spans from light tints to deep, rich shades.

Color Relationships:

Complementary Colors: Complementary colors are situated opposite each other on the color wheel, such as red and green or blue and orange. When combined, they create a striking visual contrast that enhances the vibrancy of each color.

Analogous Colors: Analogous colors are adjacent to each other on the color wheel, such as blue, green, and yellow-green. Blending analogous colors together generates a sense of harmony and unity within an arrangement.

Monochromatic Colors: Monochromatic color schemes involve various shades, tints, and tones of a single color. This approach creates a refined and cohesive aesthetic, allowing for subtle variations within a unified palette.

Creating Visual Impact:

Color Dominance: To establish a focal point in an arrangement, select one dominant color. Other colors can then be used as accents to complement and enhance the primary hue.

Color Contrast: Introducing colors with contrasting characteristics, such as warm and cool tones, adds visual intrigue and dynamism to compositions.

Color Balance: Striving for a harmonious balance entails distributing colors evenly throughout the arrangement. It is crucial to avoid overwhelming the design with an excessive number of competing hues.

Emotional and Symbolic Meanings:

Each color carries its own emotional and symbolic significance. For instance, red is often associated with passion and energy, while blue evokes a sense of calmness and tranquility. When designing a flower arrangement, it is important to consider the desired mood and message and select colors accordingly.

Incorporating Color into Flower Design:

Selecting Flowers: Explore the vast array of flowers available in various colors, taking into account their unique characteristics and symbolic meanings. By combining flowers with complementary or harmonious colors, you can create visually stunning compositions.

Texture and Form: Consider the texture and form of flowers to enhance the overall design. Some flowers possess intricate shapes and delicate petals, while others exhibit bold and architectural forms. Assess how these elements complement the chosen color palette.

Exploring Different Color Schemes:

Exploring different color schemes is a delightful way to create flower designs that are impactful and captivating. Three popular color schemes to consider are complementary, analogous, and monochromatic.

Complementary Color Scheme:

Complementary colors lie opposite each other on the color wheel. When combined, they create a striking contrast that amplifies the vibrancy of each color. To create a complementary color scheme in your flower design, select flowers that belong to opposing color pairs, such as red and green, blue and orange, or yellow and purple. The interplay between these colors will infuse your arrangement with visual dynamism and eye-catching allure.

Analogous Color Scheme:

Analogous colors reside next to each other on the color wheel. They share similar undertones, resulting in a harmonious and cohesive aesthetic when blended. To create an analogous color scheme in your flower design, choose flowers that are in close proximity on the color wheel. For example, you can select a range of flowers in shades of blue, green, and yellow-green. This color scheme will foster a sense of unity and a seamless transition of hues throughout your arrangement.

Monochromatic Color Scheme:

A monochromatic color scheme revolves around utilizing different variations of a single color. By incorporating various tints, shades, and tones of a particular color, you can achieve a sophisticated and elegant look. For instance, you can fashion a monochromatic arrangement using different shades of pink, spanning from delicate blush to deep magenta. This color scheme provides a harmonious and visually pleasing composition while highlighting the nuances within a single color family.

When working with these color schemes, it is crucial to bear in mind the principles of color dominance, contrast, and balance discussed earlier. Designate one dominant color as the focal point, employ contrasting colors to generate visual interest, and

distribute the colors evenly throughout the arrangement to achieve equilibrium.

By embracing the artistry of color theory and skillfully applying its principles, we can elevate our flower designs to new heights of beauty and expressiveness. Mastery of color opens up endless possibilities, allowing us to evoke emotions, tell stories, and create captivating arrangements that leave a lasting impression.

Seasonal floral arrangements that showcase the potential for year-round blooming

These stunning seasonal floral arrangements showcase the beauty of different seasons and provide inspiration for year-round blooming. Each arrangement captures the essence of its respective season and combines various flowers to create captivating displays. Let these arrangements ignite your creativity as you envision your own floral masterpieces throughout the year.

Spring Delights

This bouquet epitomizes the freshness of spring with pastel pink tulips, white daffodils, and fragrant hyacinths. The flowers are arranged in a glass vase adorned with fresh green moss, enhancing the delicate and vibrant blooms.

Summer Sunshine

Radiating warmth and energy, this vibrant centerpiece features a mix of sunflowers, zinnias, and daisies in shades of yellow, orange, and red. Lush greenery accents the arrangement, symbolizing the vibrant beauty of summer.

Autumn Harvest

With deep red roses, orange marigolds, and burgundy dahlias, this rustic arrangement celebrates the rich colors and textures of fall. Branches of autumn foliage and berries complement the flowers, creating a captivating display of seasonal abundance.

Winter Elegance

Sophistication defines this arrangement, which combines white roses, silver eucalyptus leaves, and icy blue delphiniums. Shimmering silver ornaments add an elegant touch, capturing the ethereal beauty of winter.

- **Spring Garden Party:**

Whimsical and romantic, this arrangement features peonies, ranunculus, and lilacs in blush pink, lavender, and soft coral hues. Cascading greenery adds a touch of elegance, evoking the joy of a spring garden party.

- **Summer Breeze:**

Channeling a cool summer breeze, this refreshing arrangement showcases blue hydrangeas, purple irises, and white lilies. Sprigs of fresh mint enhance the sense of tranquility and add a delightful fragrance.

- **Autumn Abundance:**

A bountiful centerpiece, this arrangement celebrates the abundance of autumn with vibrant orange and yellow chrysanthemums, deep red roses, and golden sunflowers. Seasonal berries and foliage provide additional accents, showcasing the richness of the season.

- **Winter Wonderland:**

Capturing the magic and serenity of a winter wonderland, this enchanting arrangement features white amaryllis, silver brunia berries, and frosted pine cones. Nestled in a bed of evergreen foliage, it exudes a sense of enchantment and beauty. Allow these descriptions to inspire your own creative endeavors and explore the possibilities of year-round blooming.

Step-by-step tutorials for creating stunning bouquets, centerpieces, and other floral designs specific to each season.

Spring Bouquet:

- Select a variety of spring blooms such as tulips, daffodils, and hyacinths in different colors.

- Trim the stems at an angle and remove any excess leaves.

- Start with a focal flower, like a large tulip or hyacinth, and hold it in your hand.

- Add smaller blooms around the focal flower, creating a spiral pattern as you go.

- Incorporate delicate filler flowers like baby's breath or wax flowers for added texture and volume.

- Add greenery, such as ferns or eucalyptus, to enhance the arrangement's natural feel.

- Secure the bouquet with floral tape or a rubber band, and wrap the stems with a ribbon or twine for a finishing touch.

Summer Centerpiece:

- Choose a mix of vibrant summer blooms like sunflowers, zinnias, and dahlias in complementary colors.

- Trim the stems at an angle and remove any foliage that will be submerged in water.

- Select a vase or container that complements the style of your arrangement.

- Start with a focal flower, like a large sunflower or dahlia, and place it in the center of the vase.

- Add smaller flowers around the focal flower, varying the heights and colors for visual interest.

- Incorporate lush greenery, such as ferns or lemon leaves, to add depth and texture to the arrangement.

- Fill any gaps with delicate filler flowers or blooms, and adjust the arrangement until you are satisfied with the overall look.

Autumn Wreath:

- Gather a variety of fall foliage, such as maple leaves, oak leaves, and branches with berries.

- Create a circular base using a wire wreath frame or a pre-made foam wreath form.

- Attach the foliage to the base using floral wire or hot glue, starting with larger leaves and working your way around the wreath.

- Add branches with berries and other seasonal elements, like pinecones or dried flowers, for additional texture and visual interest.

- Secure any loose stems or elements with additional floral wire or glue as needed.

- Hang the wreath on your front door or use it as a centerpiece by placing it on a flat surface and adding a pillar candle or a vase with seasonal flowers in the center.

Winter Table Arrangement:

- Start with a low, wide container like a shallow bowl or a decorative dish.

- Create a base using floral foam or a flower frog to hold the stems in place.

- Select wintery blooms such as amaryllis, roses, and ranunculus in shades of white, red, and deep burgundy.

- Trim the stems at an angle and insert them into the foam, starting with the focal flowers in the center.

- Add contrasting textures with foliage like pine branches, cedar, or eucalyptus leaves.

- Incorporate winter accents like silver twigs, frosted pine cones, or glittered branches for a touch of sparkle.

- Fill any gaps with smaller blooms or filler flowers like wax flowers or baby's breath.

- Place the arrangement in the center of your table and surround it with flickering candles or seasonal decor to complete the wintery ambiance.

Feel free to customize these designs by incorporating your favorite flowers, colors, and additional elements that reflect your personal style. Let your creativity blossom as you bring the beauty of each season into your home with these stunning floral creations.

Tips for Choosing Flowers, Arranging Techniques, and Creative Ideas for Seasonal Floral Designs

Selecting the Perfect Flowers:

- Consider the season: Opt for flowers that are currently in season to ensure vibrant and fresh options for your arrangements.

- Explore the symbolism: Familiarize yourself with the meanings associated with different flowers and select ones that align with the desired message or theme of your arrangement.

- Think about the color palette: Take into account the overall color scheme you want to achieve and choose flowers that harmonize with each other.

- Pay attention to fragrance: Some flowers emit delightful scents that can enhance the ambiance of your space, so consider incorporating fragrant blooms when suitable.

Arranging Techniques:

- Start with a focal point: Begin by selecting a standout flower or element that will serve as the centerpiece of your arrangement.

- Use the rule of thirds: Distribute flowers and foliage evenly throughout the arrangement, creating balance and visual interest.

- Vary heights and textures: Incorporate flowers and greenery with different heights and textures to add depth and dimension to your design.

- Consider scale and proportion: Ensure that the size of your arrangement suits the container and the space it will occupy, striking a visually pleasing balance.

- Trim and strip stems: Cut stems at an angle before placing them in water to facilitate better water absorption. Remove any excess foliage that would be submerged in water to keep it clean and prevent bacterial growth.

Creative Ideas for Seasonal Elements:

- Incorporate seasonal foliage: Use branches, leaves, or evergreen sprigs that are characteristic of the current season to add texture and depth to your arrangement.

- Integrate seasonal fruits or vegetables: Consider adding small pumpkins, gourds, or citrus fruits to fall or winter arrangements for an unexpected touch.

- Use natural elements: Explore the use of pine cones, acorns, dried wheat, or seed pods to evoke the essence of the season.

- Experiment with non-floral elements: Include feathers, ribbons, or decorative branches to bring a unique and whimsical element to your arrangement.

- Enhance with candles or lights: For evening or festive arrangements, incorporate candles or string lights to create a warm and inviting ambiance.

Remember, these tips are designed to inspire your creativity and guide you in creating beautiful seasonal floral designs. Feel free to experiment, adapt, and let your personal style shine through. Whether you're arranging flowers for a special occasion or simply adding a touch of nature to your home, let the beauty of each season guide your choices and inspire your arrangements.

CONCLUSION

Many people enjoy and find boundless satisfaction in flower gardening. But flower cultivation also has a lot of underrated advantages. In this book, you will explore all the environmental and physical benefits of flower gardening. Maintaining activity in your flower gardens has many positive health effects. More sun boosts vitamin D levels, aiding in weight reduction, mood improvement, and better sleep. Working in your flower beds and getting some sunlight can lift your spirits and improve your sleep.

Additionally, these benefits can be achieved in as little as 15 minutes a day. Flowers from the garden are elegant, appealing, and timeless. They can be used for any occasion and make for a simple yet thoughtful gift. You can create numerous floral gifts for friends and family using a variety of flowers that you cultivate yourself. The creative outlet of flower growing is accessible to most people. Planning and planting a flower garden stimulate the imagination and offer endless design options. Even a small patio area can be transformed into a beautiful botanical garden with a little work. Any outdoor space can be turned into a paradise by adding an abundance of vibrant flower pots.

Utilizing your flowers to enhance the beauty and attractiveness of your home is a significant advantage of flower cultivation. It has been shown that the mere sight of a magnificent arrangement of flowers effectively relieves stress, and their delightful scent instantly improves mood. The final advantage of flower growing is that it helps you develop a strong connection with and appreciation for nature. Flowers come in a wide variety of stunning shapes, hues, and growth patterns. They can thrive in nearly any environment and are simply gorgeous. Flower gardening will soothe your spirit, awe you with nature's wonders, and help you appreciate the creative force behind the existence of flowers. Additionally, you will encounter many flora and wildlife that adore and value flowers. From bird watching to simply enjoying the buzz of a bumblebee, your life will become richer..

REFERENCES

Stewart, A. (2007). Flower Confidential: The Good, the Bad, and the Beautiful. Algonquin Books.

Debra Prinzing (American author and pioneer of the Slow Flower movement in the US)

Erin Benzakein (brains behind the American flower farm Floret)

Terry & Katie (London-based floral studio Worm)

Amy Stewart (American author of "Flower Confidential")

PYRUS (Edinburgh-based botanical firm)

Erin Benzakein (flower grower)

Made in United States
Troutdale, OR
05/23/2024

20074753R00106